THE SECRET TO
SUCCESS

When You Want to Succeed as Bad as You Want to Breathe

Cover and Interior Design by Daryl S. Anderson Sr.
Promotional Ad Designs David Anderson

Photographers:
Cover: Karl Phillips
Studio Photo: Nicholas Brezzell

Written by Eric Thomas
Michigan State University Founder of Advantage Retention Initiative
PhD. Candidate Educational Administration
Senior Consultant of International Urban Educational Consultant
Senior Pastor Place of Change Ministries

ISBN: 978-0-9746231-0-8

THE SECRET TO
SUCCESS

When You Want to Succeed as Bad as You Want to Breathe

ERIC THOMAS

SPIRIT REIGN PUBLISHING
A Division of Spirit Reign Communications

Acknowledgements

Special Thanks BTM and BTC family: Black, Tre, Byron and George Purnell, David Richardson, James, Eric Smith, Gilbert, Ian, Kelly, Rupert Thompson, Jamal, Mason West, Big Will, T. Black (Xist entertainment) Frank Dent, Sheldon Kay, The entire West End family, Rebecca Willis, Stonophia Burrows, Tracy Fitz, Trabee, Lydia Henderson, David Arrington, Derrick Williams, Tina Riley, Geraldine Malory.

Special Thanks to The Detroit Center Church (Glenda Moseley for all your love and support, Pastor Phillip Willis and Sister Willis for your tough love, sister Burse, Elder Craig and King. Bethel Lansing for giving me my first assignment and A.P.O.C. Ministries for letting me be myself and realizing that some birds aren't meant to be caged.

Thanks for looking out: Shawn Crockwell (Bermuda Love), Patrick and Paul Graham, Marcus Flowers, Jeff Ross, Equa Epps, Gama(s) (Bernie, Bam Bam, Keaton, Al, Lonny, Shawn, Angelo & Byron Scott) and Maurice Gordon, Davion Fouche, the Graham crew (Camille, Dave, and Michele), and the Raw Dogs (Rodney Cooper, and Jeff Wilder).

OC West Wings for life: Mo from the N.O. (New Orleans), Jeff Harley (Atlantic City), Gerald Pennick (L.A.), Christian (Oklahoma), Henry and Curtis (Birmingham).

Educators: Henry Ford High Mrs. Nun

Oakwood Elder Shan the Man, Dr. Barnes, Dr. Janice Johnson, Dr. Evelyon Johnson, Coach Roddy, Dr. and sister Paul, Trevor Frazier, President and first lady Baker, Deborah Fryson

Michigan State University Rodney Patterson, Murray Edwards, Dr. Chris Dunbar, Dr. Bonita Curry, Dr. Lee June, Dr. Sonia Gunnings, Dr. Pero Dagbovie, Dr. Susan Printy and Dr. Nancy Coldflesh.

And sincere thanks to All my Haters. Your negativity and criticism continues to push me and challenge me to reach new levels of greatness.

Dedication

This book is dedicated to:

Vernessa and Jesse Thomas (mom & dad). Thanks for being courageous enough to be my parents and not my friends. I can see clearly now the rain is gone (meaning, I have children of my own... lol).

De De Moseley (the love of my life). Thanks for being the other piece of iron that sharpens me and for being the wind beneath my wings.

I will Love you always:

Jeneco and Malori (lil sisters)

Jalen and Jayda (my seeds)

Ladies of my life:
Grandma Gwen, Grandma Lama, Auntie Wanda, Auntie Cleo, Auntie Booby, Auntie Tawana for your continued support since diapers. Sister Lamb, Ma Trotter and Ma Bez (Sterline Foster)

Men of my life:
Unlce Bruce, Uncle Jimmy, Tim and Wayne Smith, Robert King, Leon Burnette, Pastor James Doggette, T. Marshall Kelly, Preston Turner, Rupert Cannonier, Clift Kyle, Renee Chandler, Steve, Pastor James Black, Elder Ward and E. E. Cleveland

Accountability Brothers:
LaDon Daniels, Lee Lamb, Lloyd Paul (S/O St. Marteen), Carlas

Quinney, Burks Hollands, Shannon Austin, Greg Arneaud, Adrian Marsh, Derrick Green, Quest Green, Joey Kibble, Karl Phillips.

Oakwood legends who inspired me:
Dennis Ross III, Virtue (mad love for the Trotter sisters) and Shavon Floyd, Sharon Riley and Faith Chorale, Charles Arrington, Angelic Clay, Angela Brown, Brian McKnight, W.S.B. (Willing Succeeding and Black) DP (Owen Simmons), Voice of Triumph (Damien Chandler), Whitney Phips, Barry Black, Chris Willis, Take 6, Dajuan Starling, and Connect Four.

Contents

Section III
The Secret 2 My Success

Foreword

This is an excellent book, written by a person with a profoundly relevant message. The message is inspirational, motivational, and timely. It is inspirational because it is a message of resiliency, hope, and success. It is motivational because it leads the reader to see that success is possible; that one can overcome odds; and that what appear to be setbacks can be building blocks. It is timely because there is a need today, and in all ages, for a message of hope for all, but particularly for our youth and aspiring high school and college students.

I remember vividly meeting Mr. Thomas (Eric) when he first gave his presentation at Michigan State University. The presentation was well received and I said to myself- "This is a person with a message". The message that day was one of honesty, hope, survival, resiliency and yes-motivational. So well received, he was invited back to campus numerous times. As I have come to know and respect Mr. Thomas over the years, I can now say that he is not just a motivational speaker, but someone with a life story that motivates. He walks the talk and practices what he "preaches".

I recommend this book to all. While autobiographical

and gripping in the story it tells, it is also filled with success and life tips. This is what I really like about the book. The tips are born out of life experiences and presented in a way that is appealing, gripping, and educational.

The book is a must read for those seeking inspiration and hope; for those looking for a tool to instill inspiration and hope; and for high school and college students who are aspiring for success in the midst of what seems like obstacles. It could also be used as part of a curriculum to teach much needed life skills and success principles.

The book presents Mr. Thomas' story only up to a certain point in his life. He continues to be a person of inspiration to many across the nation. I thank and congratulate him for this contribution via this book, and expect much more from him in the future. As it has been said- "To whom much is given, much is required". To Mr. Thomas (Eric), much has been given and experienced, and thus it is required of you to share with us and to continue to walk in integrity.

Lee N. June, Ph.D.

Professor

Michigan State University

Formerly Served as Vice President for Student Affairs and Services and Associate Provost for Academic Student Services and Multicultural Issues.

August 2011

SECTION

I

THE STRUGGLE

THE SECRET TO SUCCESS

CHAPTER

1

Boiling Point

"Anger is a wind which blows out the lamp of the mind."
Robert Green Ingersoll

"I hate you!" I wish I could take back the words I said to her that day, but I couldn't. I swear it was not premeditated. If I could only turn back the hands of time, I would have done it differently. I should have sat her down years ago and just talked it out. I should have gotten it out of my system instead of being so secretive about it. I should have told her the day it happened that I felt betrayed and angry, and that I felt as though I couldn't trust her anymore. Why didn't I just tell her? Well, it's too late; I have gone too far. I can't go back and change things now. It is what it is!

<<Ring…ring…ring>>. "Hello…hello," I said as I rolled over in the bed reaching for the phone.

"What you still doing in the bed?" Melvin said in a surprised tone.

"What? It's Sunday, it's cold, football season is over, and I have the house to myself. Unless you know something I don't, I don't see a reason to get outta bed! The question is, why are you calling my house so early? Don't you got a girl yet?", I asked jokingly as I readjusted the covers.

"I'm lifting weights and I need someone to spot me," Melvin replied.

"Why didn't you say that in the first place? Give me thirty. I need to hop in the shower real quick and throw some gear on." I jumped out of the bed, grabbed a pair of all red Lathrup High jogging pants, my red Lathrup hoodie, a pair of socks, a white t-shirt, my underwear, and headed for the bathroom.

Suddenly, I heard a noise coming from downstairs. It sounded like someone opening the garage door, but that was impossible. My parents were in Chicago visiting my aunt Wanda. Then I heard loud footsteps moving toward the living room. My heart was pounding so loud I was afraid the intruder could hear it. My adrenaline started to kick in and I tiptoed back into my room, grabbed my baseball bat from under my bed, and headed toward the stairs. With the bat tightly clinched in both hands, I gently walked down each stair trying desperately not to make a sound. As I approached the last step, I turned my body toward the direction where I heard the sound and out of the corner of my eye I saw a large male frame standing in the living room area. I walked slowly toward the figure with the bat at my side, ready to swing and bring whoever it was to the ground. I bent down trying to stay low when suddenly, the image became clear. It was my father. But that could not be, he was supposed to be in Chicago with my mother. I stopped dead in my tracks, did an about face, and ran back up the stairs. With each step my heart pounded harder and harder. Once I made it to the top of the stairs I shot into my room, grabbed the phone and called Melvin back. "Dog, you're not going to believe this my father's at the crib!" "I thought you said they were in Chicago," Melvin asked. "I thought they were too, but apparently he's not. I think he's been here the entire weekend." "Alright, calm down, just calm down, whatever you do don't panic, just act normal. He probably doesn't even know," Melvin whispered. "You right, I put all the beer bottles in the garbage, put everything back like I found it and I cleaned the house pretty good. You're right, I'm trippin, he didn't notice. We did trash all the bottles and clean the grill, right?" Melvin was quiet.

Once I got off the phone with Melvin I quickly hopped in the shower. When I got out I threw on my jogging pants and hoodie, headed down the stairs and out the door. I was half way out of the door when suddenly I heard him call my name. "Eric, do you know what your mother did with the steak?" "What steak?" I replied without hesitation. I headed toward the kitchen trying to keep a straight face. I kept thinking about what Melvin said, "Stay calm and act like nothing happened." "Are you sure you have no idea what your mother did with the steak?" "Yes sir, she didn't mention anything to me about no steak." "All right," he said. "I'm about to go over Melvin's for a while." I walked out of the door slowly as to suggest everything was normal, but I knew if they found out I threw a party at the house and barbequed the steak, I was a dead man walking. I had a feeling my father didn't buy my story and as soon as my mom got home from Chicago he was going to check with her to find out what really happened. If they put all the pieces together, I was going to have to get out of the house before my father killed me.

"Stop being so paranoid. You know how mean your old dude is, if he thought for one second we had a party at the house last night, he would have murdered you by now," Melvin said jokingly. "You haven't said a word since you been here. For real E, you need to chill out. Tomorrow morning everything will be back to normal." <<Ring... ring...>> "Hello, how are you?" Melvin's mom said as she picked up the phone.

I got quiet and went to the stairwell so I could hear Mrs. Brown's conversation. I can't explain it, but somehow I just knew that it was my mother on the other end of the phone. My heart started racing again. It was early evening and that was around the time my mom generally made it in whenever she drove home from Chicago. Also, the tone in Melvin's mother's voice didn't sound like she was speaking to a close friend.

"As a matter of fact they were together late last night," she told the person on the other end. "Not a problem, have a good evening, I'll talk to you soon." "Eric, that was your mother, she wants you to come home."

"I knew it! I knew it. I shouldn't have listened to you. I knew I shouldn't have thrown a party at the crib," I said while pacing the floor. "We probably left all kind of evidence. Man, he is about to kill me. I knew I shouldn't have listened to ya'll fools."

"Stop acting like a punk and calm down. You want me to go with you?"

Trying to impress Melvin, I lied, "Naw, I ain't scared of that dude. Let me get my jacket. I'm good. I'll call you if I need you."

"You know I got your back," Melvin said sincerely.

Even though I knew he had my back, I was not in the least bit comforted by his words. He didn't have to face my father, I did. On the way home I cut through the neighbor's yard taking my usual shortcut, but then backtracked and took the scenic route. It didn't make a lot of sense to rush home for a butt whipping. As I walked toward the house I told myself, "Party or no party, right or wrong, he wasn't going to put his hands on me again." I was the only kid on the block still getting whippings in high school. I was 16 and still had to wear long-sleeved shirts to school to hide the bruises on my arm that I got from trying to protect myself from the belt. It actually looked worse than it felt.

What hurt the most was the fact that my classmates would joke on me about it. When I walk in this house if any one of them says something about me getting a whipping, it's on!

As I grabbed the knob on the screen door and walked through the garage into the house, I kept telling myself to relax and act normal. I deliberately went through the garage and not the front door because it gave me a few extra minutes to gather myself. I paused for about 30 seconds to calm down, gain my composure, and practice saying, "What's up ma, Mrs. Brown said you wanted to talk to me." I must have practiced saying, "What up ma, Mrs. Brown said you wanted to talk to me," a million times before I mustered up enough courage to walk into the house, and into the family room to face my parents. As I walked into the family room, the sight of my parents struck fear in my heart. I opened my mouth and all the moisture evaporated and my voice began to crack, "Mrs. Bbbbbbrown, I stuttered, ssssaid you wanted to see me."

"Yes, I talked with your dad yesterday and he said that the steak was missing. Do you know what happened to it?

"No ma'am."

"Well, that's strange because your father and I found beer bottles in the backyard and the grill looks like someone cooked steak on it recently. I am going to try this again! Did you have a party here last night?" she pressed.

"Party? No ma'am, I didn't have a party here last night." I tried to keep a straight face, but it was difficult because my mom always knew when I was lying.

"Stop lying. Eric, I am so damn sick of you. How could you have a party in my house, eat the groceries your father and I worked for, and have absolute strangers in my house? What in the hell were you thinking?" she screamed. I didn't say a word; I just stared at her.

"Eric, do you hear me talking to you? I asked you a question, what in the hell were you thinking? I want an answer and I want it now!" I didn't flinch, I just stood there with a blank look on my face.

"Son, your mother asked you a question," he chimed in. I pretended as if I did not hear a word he was saying. "I know you hear me talking to you son…I said your mother asked you a question!" He typically used a different tone of voice when he had to repeat himself. He was from the old school and believed that when an adult spoke to a child, the child was supposed to acknowledge he or she was being spoken to. I knew the drill. If you did not respond the first time, he would ask you a second time a bit louder, giving you the benefit of the doubt that maybe you didn't hear him. He was not necessarily trying to scare you by projecting his voice; it was more of a warning. Generally, I would surrender. I would play the dumb role like I did not hear him the first time, and the second time say, "yes sir" and answer the question. Not this time. In a strong and demanding voice he said, "Boy, you better answer your mother." Before I knew it I snapped and my mind went blank. I was physically in the room, but mentally I was long gone.

"You can't make me," I murmured under my breath as I bit my bottom lip and shook my head as if to say "not this time—not this time."

I knew what I was doing was dangerous. I had heard stories of how his 6 foot 8 inch 250 pound frame had annihilated men twice my size, but I was tired of living in fear. Before I knew it, I was racing toward him in an attempt to get past him and into the garage. But as I made my initial move out of the family room toward the hallway he blocked the pathway and moved in on me. He had an obvious advantage in both reach and size but I thought I could offset it with my quickness. I launched toward him in an attempt to knock him down and give me enough time to run through the hallway toward the door leading to the garage. As I went to push him, he grabbed my arm and before I knew it had me in a headlock gasping for air. I tried to use my lower body strength to force his legs from under his body, but it didn't work. The next thing I knew he was hitting me with some serious blows to the body. Helpless, the only thing I could think to do was pray. I didn't go to church and I was definitely not a Christian, but I figured I had nothing to lose by calling on Him. "God if you can hear me—Help! This dude is about to kill me!" Within in a matter of seconds, I was able to push both of his arms toward his body and loosen the cobra-like grip he had me in. I began to pull my head back in an attempt to regain my balance. The only thing I wanted to do was try to create enough separation between us so that I could make it out of the house. Once I was completely free from his grip I pushed him away and ran toward the garage. I made it safely into the washroom and slammed the door shut behind me to give myself a few extra seconds. I ran through the garage and exited the door to the far left. I figured he would go through the front door and try to cut me off but I was too quick; by the time I made it out of the garage, I noticed he and my mother were just getting to the porch. Once I made it to the street I knew I was in the clear because there was no way either one of them could catch me. I stopped running once I made it past the mailbox and into the street. I turned and faced my mother. All I remember thinking was, I waited four years to say this. It was late in the afternoon, and as luck would have it, on this particular Sunday, it seemed like all our neighbors were outside. It felt like a scene out of a movie. All the neighbors stopped what they were doing and all eyes were on our family. Tears began rolling down my face uncontrollably and I exploded, "I hate you, I swear to God I hate you! You watched him put his hands on me and you didn't do nothin'. You never said nothin' to him. You should have protected me! I hate you!"

My mother yelled back at me but I was in such a haze I couldn't hear anything but my rapid heartbeat. "You put him before me, you put him before your own blood," I shouted. Then he interrupted in an attempt to put his two cents in. "Who you talking to?" he growled.

"Shut up talking to me! You don't mean nothin' to me! If I see you in the streets, I'm killin' you!" The neighbors looked on in astonishment with their mouths wide open. We lived in a diverse community at the time and it was quiet for the most part. Lathrup Village (the suburbs) was the complete opposite of our old neighborhood on the west side of Detroit. In Detroit, it was nothing to hear sirens racing through the hood in the middle of the night, or the sound of bass pounding out of the local drug dealer's car as they drove up and down the block.

By no means were we the Huxtables. We had our challenges, but I don't think any of us ever thought it would come to this. Just before I took off running, I stopped everything and stared at my mom thinking, "How could you betray me? How could you put your husband before your own son? How could you keep that secret from me all those years?"

CHAPTER

2

Sweet Little Lies

"I'm sorry mama I never meant to hurt you. I never meant make you cry but tonight, I'm cleaning out my closet." – Eminem

My body felt numb. In my anger, I said things I never thought I'd say to the one person I loved more than life. I never intended to hurt my mom. I guess I held it in so long that when it finally came out; it came out with no regard for anything or anyone.

Tears ran down my face as I thought, "Not in a million years did I ever think that my mom would lie to me. It hurt my heart watching her stand there on the porch next to him after he just tried to kill me. It was like she was saying, "No matter what, right or wrong, I am going to support my husband and I don't care how you feel." Never in my wildest dreams did I think she could do or say anything to hurt me as much as when she kept the secret from me. I was wrong, this hurt just as much.

Once I snapped out of my trance, I realized I had to make a decision, and I had to make it quick. The question was, *"Do I run to my right, east towards Telegraph Road, or do I run towards the left, west towards Lasher Road?"* I decided to run west.

It all happened so fast. I wasn't quite sure where I was headed and to be honest it didn't matter as long as I was getting the hell away from them. When I got to the end of the block, I kept straight and ran through the neighbor's yard to Ivanhoe Lane. I wanted to make sure my father couldn't trace my steps. I kept running until I no longer recognized where I was. After I passed a liquor store on 11 Mile and Lahser, I noticed an empty field behind the houses. As I got closer to the field I discovered that it was a small park. The park had a few pieces of playground equipment: a swing set, monkey bars, and a metal rippled slide all enclosed by sand. I sat down on the edge of the slide trying to catch my breath. Once I regained my composure, I walked over to the swing set and began swinging. I tried not to think about the day I found out, but it was impossible.

It was a Catch-22. On one hand, I wanted to know the truth, but on the other hand, I was afraid. As far back as I could remember, certain family members tried to convince me that my mother was keeping something from me. I was really strong in the beginning; whenever someone would slightly hint about my mom and some family secret, I would dismiss it because of the ultimate trust I had in her. As the years passed, something was eating at me. I couldn't take not knowing any longer. I took matters into my own hands.

As I approached the hallway leading into my parent's room, I heard my conscious say, *"Eric, don't do it, you know you shouldn't go into your parent's room looking through their personal belongings. If you really want to know, just call your mom and ask."* I stopped for a quick second to acknowledge the voice, but like so many other times before, I ignored it. I walked out of the hallway and slowly into their room passed the bed and toward their dresser. I couldn't decide if what I was looking for was in their armoire or the dresser and didn't have all day to decide. My father was a supervisor at GM; which meant he could pop in at any moment. I stood there for about 30 seconds when suddenly, a light came on, *"Eeny, meeny, miny, moe."* My index finger was pointing at the honey pine finished dresser when I got to the last moe. I walked toward the dresser and cautiously opened the top left drawer. I wanted to make sure no one else knew I had been in the drawer, so I memorized sure where everything was so I could put things back exactly how I found them. When I opened the drawer, I also noticed a sliver box with a lock. It looked like something my parents would keep important papers in, but I didn't know how much time I had, so I moved it to the side and began looking through the papers in the top drawer. I grabbed the first set of papers and my hands began shaking. As I looked through them, I didn't see anything, so I began putting them on the top of the dresser sequentially so I would not forget what order they were in. After a few minutes of looking and finding nothing relevant, I began feeling bad for going through their things. All I saw was a bunch of junk mail and old receipts. Just as I was about to close the drawer and get out of Dodge, I noticed a piece of paper that looked like a birth certificate. I stared at it for a minute, debating if I really wanted to look at it. As I grabbed it with my right hand, my heart sank in my chest. I pulled it close to my face and studied it like an exam. The first thing I noticed was the city in which I was born. That section had Chicago, my mother's maiden name, and my father's name. The birth certificate seemed legit. It had the official State of Illinois insignia and the words, Certificate of Live Birth, in bold letters. The first section had my name, Eric Douglas Thomas, my birth date and the hour I was born. The second section showed my sex, and the county I was born in. The third line seemed legit as well. It indicated that I was born in Chicago, within city limits. Everything seemed cool until I got to the parent section. First, it listed my mom's name, her age at the time of my birth, and the city she resided in. From the look of it, my father's information was correct as well, but something seemed a little strange. My father's section didn't even contain the **relation to child** question. He just signed his name under father's name. My mom's section had the question clearly spelled out—*relation to the child, mother.* The other red flag was the section that asked for their ages. I knew for certain that there was a four-year age difference between my parents. So I did the math, at 18 my mom was living in Chicago finishing school at Dunbar High and my father was in college at Texas Southern playing basketball. Come to think of it, my father was from Detroit, he never even lived in Chicago. So if he lived in Detroit, and my mom lived in Chicago, if she was in high school, and he was in college, they couldn't have possibly known each other. To make it worse, I already knew they weren't married at the time I was born. I started to feel light headed and my heart started racing faster and faster and I started sweating. I couldn't believe what I was seeing. I started telling myself, "Maybe they were shocked when they found out my mom was pregnant and didn't know what to do. Or maybe they were too young to get married and needed more time to figure out what they wanted to do." I tried to come up with every reason I could to justify what was happening. The only thing left for me to do was to call my mom. "Yeah, I'll call my mom and she'll straighten all this out." I picked up the phone and quickly dialed her work number. "Microfilm," she said in her professional voice. "Mom, I need to ask you a question!" She could tell something was wrong in my voice. "What is it son?" "If I ask you will you promise to tell me the truth?" I said in a real nervous tone. "I promise, now what is it?" she asked.

"Is daddy my real father?" The silence penetrated my soul. It might have only lasted for a few seconds, but it felt like minutes. Finally she said, "No son, he isn't your real father."

CHAPTER

3

I'm a Survivor

Now that you are out of my life, I'm so much better, You thought that I'd be weak without ya', But I'm stronger, You thought that I'd be broke without ya, But I'm richer, You thought that I'd be sad without ya', I laugh harder, You thought I wouldn't grow without ya', Now I'm wiser, You thought that I'd be helpless without ya, But I'm smarter, You thought that I'd be stressed without ya', But I'm chillin'
---Destiny's Child

As the sun started to set, I got nervous. Although this wasn't my first time being away from home, it was the first time I left home and didn't have a clue as to where I was going. The darker it got, the more unsettled I was. Somehow, the anger I felt from the situation that took place earlier between me and my parents vanished. Fear of the unknown had replaced the feelings of anger and any other emotion I had at that time. I felt overwhelmed every time I thought about where I was going to sleep and what I was going to eat. I got nauseous thinking about how long it might be before I had a normal life again. It began to hit me that I never thought the whole thing through. I let my emotions get the best of me. Just as the words, "I shouldn't have" were coming out of my mouth, I heard my inner-voice say, "Humble yourself and go back home, apologize and deal with the consequences. If you go back, the punishment will be harsh but they will forgive you." "I can't, I can't do it," I kept repeating. I started scratching my head and rubbing my face to clear my thoughts. I couldn't believe I allowed that thought to enter my mind. I decided from that point forward, no matter how terrified I was, no matter how lonely I was, no matter how hurt I was or how defeated I felt, I was not going back. I made a vow to myself that day, "Today I will live as a free man and never return home."

From this point forward I had to take care of myself. I saw things like this on National Geographic. One day a cub sits by watching the mother lioness intensively staring down its prey, and at the prime moment, attacks, devours, and shares her kill with the cub. A few months later it's a different situation entirely. The cub routinely follows his mother just as he had in the past. In the back of his mind he's thinking, dinner will be served in a few short minutes. He watches his mother stare at her prey and wait for the opportunity to attack. Finally, she makes her move and begins to run at top speed. As she approaches her victim, she launches in the air onto the back of her prey and forces it to the ground. Once on the ground, the lioness cuts the victim's throat with the nails from her claws. As the lioness begins to devour her kill, the young cub moves in closer and waits for his mother to rip off a healthy portion of meat to share, but to his surprise the lioness turns on him as if he were an enemy. In that moment, the cub realizes he must hunt his own prey if he is to eat again.

It was about 8:45pm—pitch-black, and reality was setting in. I was homeless. The whole day was like a blur and I was in a daze; it was as if I was paralyzed. Every time I thought about moving, the strangest thing happened: when I tried to walk, I was literally stuck. I said to myself, "Eric, you need to go someplace where it's warm, someplace safe, but every time I tried to take a step forward nothing happened. I heard a voice whisper in my ear, "You messed up real bad this time. What are you going to do now, huh? You just going to sit there and do nothing, is that it?" "Every time you're in a crunch, like a little punk, you freeze up. You wanted to be a grown man well you are grown now. Ain't nobody going to bail you out this time!" As hard as it was to listen to those words, I knew they were real. Like the cub, I was on my own. Suddenly, I stood up tall, lifted my head, wiped the tears from my eyes, and cleared my thoughts. By this time it was a little past 9:30 pm, and there were a few things I knew for sure. The weekend was over and I had school the next day; I needed to decide where I was going to sleep and how I was going to eat.

I don't' ever remember a time before this situation that I was eager to be in school. It's funny how one situation can change your whole perspective. Now, I was eager to get to school in the morning. When I walked out the front door of Lathrup High School that Friday afternoon, school was the last thing on my mind. Other than recess, lunch and track and field, I didn't care too much for it. I was already pissed off because my parents moved us out of Detroit to the suburbs. One day out of the blue my parents told me that I would not be returning to Detroit Henry Ford High School. They told me I would be attending Southfield Lathrup. I had gone to the neighborhood schools since I was in the first grade, first McKinney, Taft, and then Ford. I couldn't believe they could be so selfish. What was I supposed to do, just start all over in the 11th grade? Maybe my parents would have been justified; sending me to a new school in my freshmen year, but to do it during my junior year was unacceptable. I had experienced eight years of bonding with friends, and all that went down the drain because my parents wanted to move to the suburbs. Going from a predominately black school to a predominately white school created some unique challenges. There were few black teachers and it was obvious that the white teachers were not accustomed to dealing with black students, especially black males. I was in the principal's office on a regular basis for either disrupting the class or insubordination. Not to mention the fact that I was having some major academic challenges changing from the Detroit Public School curriculum to Southfields Public School curriculum. Lathrup's academic pace was ten times faster than Detroit's. I hardly ever had homework at Henry Ford and rarely had more than one test a week. I had homework on a regular basis at Lathrup and it was nothing for three or more teachers to give tests the same week. I hated everything about Lathrup, the faculty and staff, the academics, and on top of that their athletic program was terrible.

Just three days ago the only reason I wanted to be in school was for the girls, field trips, or a pep rally. Now I couldn't wait for the doors to open. I needed to get out of the cold and get into a place where I felt safe. But first, I needed a place to lay my head that was in walking distance of my bus route. There was a stop near Melvin's house, which seemed perfect at first, but I was somewhat leery because my parents knew where Melvin lived and would almost certainly check for me there. "Don't even think about it," I said to myself before I could finish my next thought. Have you lost your mind?" I knew it was risky. It would be secluded enough so that no one would know I was there, but close enough to Melvin's house that if something happened, I could run to his house for help.

I stood there for a few seconds trying to convince myself that getting up from my spot behind the park to head toward my final destination for the night was worth it. It was more difficult than it sounded because even though it was officially spring, somehow the sun didn't get the message. Michigan's weather is weird like that; it might be in the upper 50's during the day and drop to the lower 20's by nightfall. The first few steps were hard. The last thing I wanted to do, especially on an empty stomach, was walk another mile. When I first stood up, I couldn't feel my legs and I was fatigued, but a surge of energy kicked in. I took my hands out of my navy Eastbay lettermen jacket and sped up my pace. I passed the Synagogue on Lahser Rd. and was approaching Melvin's street, Ivanhoe. I thought about stopping for quick second, but knew I didn't need to get sidetracked. While walking I couldn't help but think how in less than 24 hours my whole world had turned upside down. I went from living a middle-class life style, which consisted of having my own room, wearing the latest gear, going to upscale restaurants, traveling every now and again, having my own car, to being homeless. It felt like a bad dream but I knew it was much deeper than a dream this time. After walking more than an hour, I had made it. It had been a long day and I was ready to get some sleep. But something in my spirit was saying take a peek through the window of the house to make sure no one is up. As I had expected, the lights were off and it appeared that my parents were asleep. I figured the backyard of my parent's house would be the safest place for me to lay my head until I could find some place better. My survival instincts kicked in and I went to my neighbor's patio and borrowed their sofa cushions from their patio set. There were big bushes in our yard that sat a few inches from the house. I figured if I slept between the wall and the bushes no one would see me. Once my bed was situated, I put my arms through my shirt to keep warm and placed my coat over me. As I lay there trying to fall asleep, I noticed how gorgeous the sky was. It had a deep black coat that made the stars shine brightly. I began to whisper a short prayer. "God, I don't know if you really exist, but if you do and you can hear me, I need some help. Please keep me safe tonight, forgive me of all the things I have done wrong, Amen."

"When I was a child, I talked like a child, I thought like a child, I reasoned like a child. When I became a man, I put childish ways behind me."
1 Corinthians 13:11

SECTION

II

THE SOLUTION

CHAPTER

4

Change Starts With You

"Everyone thinks of changing the world, but no one thinks of changing himself" - **Leo Tolstoy**

For four long years I dreamt about it, I talked about, I longed for it. I told myself, "Just hold on, it won't be long— 18 will be here soon.   By then you will have graduated from high school, moved out of the house, and you will be on your way to college. Once you go to college you don't ever have to go back home." I guess I was lucky because my wish came true two years before my 18th birthday. There was only one problem; I left home with nowhere to go. What should have been a celebration of my independence turned out to be a nightmare. How could I have been so stupid? I literally slammed the door and walked out of a four-bedroom, two and a half bath, fully furnished, stocked refrigerator, 2,700 square foot home, and ran into the horrifying emptiness of sleepless nights, begging for food, and eating out of trashcans. Wisdom calls for one to compare what he is giving up with what he is gaining. In my case, I gained absolutely nothing.

Principle 1: Don't make a habit out of choosing what feels good over what's actually good for you.

When I stormed out of the house that day my father looked me in my face and said, "Eric, you better think about what you're about to do because if you walk out of this house right now, if you walk out of that door, you're saying to me that you're a grown man. So let me make myself clear, if you leave, you will never come back to this house. Do I make myself clear?" I was so fed up with him and the way he treated me that I wasn't even phased by his statement. I would be the first to admit that when things didn't go my way I reacted off of anger and emotion. Because of that I landed myself in an awful situation.

Let's do an exercise. If I told you I would give you 10 million dollars to jump out of a Boeing 757 aircraft with no parachute, what would you say? If you answered no, I am not mad at you. I would have given the same answer at one point in time. "Even though I could really use 10 million dollars right now, it does me no good if I'm dead." But for those of you who answered no, you would be very disappointed when you found out that the aircraft was not 30, 000 feet above sea level. That's right, the monstrous machine never left the ground and the jump down would be about 6 feet. Consider all factors before making a decision, ask as many questions as you can about the situation. I have learned over the years that the higher the level of emotion, the lower the level of reasoning. For example, if your emotions are at the highest level of 10, your ability to reason is at a 0. If it's a 9 then your reasoning is a 1. I am not suggesting that emotions don't have their place, but taking actions based purely on emotions is dangerous and could cost you everything.

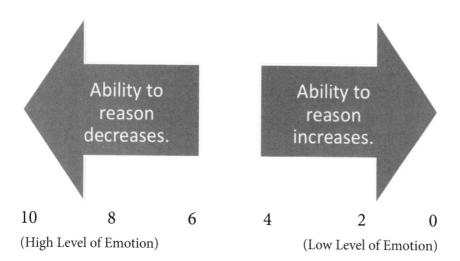

| 10 | 8 | 6 | 4 | 2 | 0 |
| (High Level of Emotion) | | | | (Low Level of Emotion) | |

Principle 2: Avoid being your own enemy.

What's holding you back? You - not anyone else.

At age 13 Tim was like an older brother to me. He was responsible for helping me earn my "Street Credit." The process was similar to what is known in the African culture as, rites of passage, or in the Jewish community as Bar Mitzvah. Once a male reached puberty on our block, he officially crossed over into a new world. The first couple years it was all about the bravado and the ladies. Tim stressed this one point, "Don't ever be the person to start a fight, but you better damn sure finish it." From that day on until I was about 14, Tim, his brother Wayne, and the rest of guys on the block beat the brakes off me until they felt I was capable of handling my own in a brawl. Of all the lessons Tim imparted on me, he was most proud that he personally schooled me on how to be a lady's man. He gave me a full anatomy lecture, which included the extended version of the birds and the bees. In addition to the lecture, we watched a few "birds and the bees for dummies" demonstration videos. I think the first few demo videos were, *Deep Throat and Debbie does Dallas.*

I'm not sure why I didn't think to call Tim when the whole thing first went down. I guess I was trying to work things out on my own. It didn't take long before I realized I was in trouble and needed some help. I called Tim to see if I could stay with him until I got on my feet. "Tim, what up, it's E.T. I know I haven't hollered at you in a minute, but I am in a bind and I need you." He didn't hesitate, "What you need bro?' "I need a place to lay my head for a while until I get on my feet." "What happened? You and your father got into it again?" he said in a disappointed tone. "Yeah, but this time I am not going back, I can't deal with that mess anymore!" "Where are you now, I am on my way." Tim lived in his own two-bedroom apartment off Woodward Avenue in the Palmer Park area. Talk about a dream becoming a reality, it was the perfect scenario. Total freedom. I could come and go as I pleased and I wouldn't have to worry about doing any chores. However, I think Tim envisioned things a bit differently. I remember our first conversation a few days after I moved in. Tim said, "Lil bro, you are a grown ass man now, so I am going to treat you like one. I am going to say this one time and one time only, if you handle your business everything between us will be fine, but if not...." He gave me the look. "Number one, you will finish school and you better not miss one day of school unless you are deathly ill. This is a no skipping zone. Two, I work and I don't have time to run back and forth to your school because of your behavior. If you get in trouble, you are on your own. Three, I'll pay the rent, I'll pay the phone bill, I'll pay the electricity, but E, I cannot feed you bro. You are going to have to get a part time job so you can take care of your own personal needs. Oh and I am going to need you to find somewhere else to crash from time to time. I can't have you in the crib when I bring my chicks through. I know it's a two bedroom, but it's also a bachelor pad. When you see a red shoestring hanging on the door outside, come back in the morning so you can shower before school."

Not two months after the conversation, Tim kicked me out. Tim was a police officer, so he was hardly home. With no adult supervision, I reverted back to the old E.T. I had no interest in school so it was a challenge to get up every morning at 5:30 a.m. and getting dressed in time to catch the 6:30 a.m. bus. Some days I pretended I went to school. I got up, got dressed, and hung out in the hood until it was time to come home. I had far less discipline than I did when I lived in my parents' house and my interest in school was hitting an all time low.

Principle 3: *You can change environments, but until you change yourself nothing else will ever change.*

I had the fresh start I dreamed of when I moved in with Tim. Somehow I thought that shifting addresses would magically change my situation. I ended up taking Tim for granted in much the same way I took my parents for granted. I never washed the dishes or cleaned up after myself. When Tim brought women home the house always smelled like trash and dirty dishes. I was being classic Eric Thomas. Same process—same exact outcome. I got kicked out my parent's house; I got kicked out of Tim's house.

Summary: Principles 1-3

- **Principle 1: Don't make a habit out of choosing what feels good over what's actually good for you.**

- **Principle 2: Avoid being your own enemy.**

- **Principle 3: You can change environments, but until you change yourself nothing else will ever change.**

CHAPTER

5

Where Do I Start?

"Though no one can go back and make a brand new start, anyone can start from now and make a brand new ending." - **Carl Bard**

As we go into the next few chapters, we're going to talk about change for obvious reasons. If there is one lesson we can take away so far it's that change doesn't happen by osmosis. However, I want to demystify the concept of change. Too often I hear individuals speak about change as if it's not something that can be attained and that it's extremely complex. The truth is that change is simple, but it's not easy. So let me be the first to encourage you. If I can do it, anybody can do it. But remember, the first thing we have to do is stop comparing change to some complex coordinates in the theory of atomic and molecular structure and dynamics. It's not that deep. As a matter of fact, change is so simple that even a child can do it.

Principle 4: *Learn to be curious.*

Symbolically, when I look at change and think about the initial process, I think about the genie in the bottle story. The story begins with a scared, angry young man walking up and down the beach. While walking, he notices a beautiful golden bottle. His curiosity drives him to move closer. He bends down and picks up the bottle. Once in his grasp he begins to rub it. To his surprise, "BOOM!" the genie appears. "Thank you for setting me free. For thousands of years I have been trapped inside this bottle waiting to be released to share with someone the secrets to success. And to show you my appreciation, you may ask me for anything, and your wish is my command."

Don't miss the message. For many of us our change has been bottled up. I believe within every person is the capacity for change. Furthermore, I believe every individual at some point in his or her life has had multiple opportunities to change. The reality is, many of us do not recognize the need for change or understand the principles needed to create change in our lives. One group of individuals think that they do not need to change and that everybody else needs to change. The second group believes that change is connected to location. If only they could relocate. If only they could move to another city, state, or even country, life would be so much better. We will use the story of the genie to reveal some of the most vital secrets to unleashing the power of change in each of our lives.

Principle 5: *Don't be afraid to explore your curiosity.*

What if I told you that the first step in experiencing real success does not require any painstaking effort at all? That's right; the first step in the process only requires a little exploration of your curiosity. Webster defines curiosity as "a strong desire to know or learn something." I know it sounds too good to be good to be true, but honestly, the day my luck and my life changed for the better had absolutely nothing to do with effort. Before I left home, I was minding my own business, living life the best way I knew how to live it when all of a sudden, I found myself sleeping in abandoned buildings, eating out of trashcans, and stealing food from the local grocery stores. I remember thinking to myself, "I don't know how I got here, and I damn sure don't know how to get myself out." In my distress, a thought popped in my head, *"What would have to happen in order for you to get out of this mess?"* I spent the next few days thinking just that, trying to figure out in my mind what it would take to get from this point in my life to where I knew I was destined to be.

Follow the story carefully, it was curiosity and curiosity alone that drove that scared, angry young man toward the beautiful bottle, and it was the exploration of that desire that caused him to rub it. As a result, the genie was set free and the scared, angry, young man was thrust into his new season. Pay attention to the initial exchange between the young man and the genie. Nowhere in the story does the genie ask for a large sum of money or even a small down payment to activate the change process. Let's be honest, that is not our experience. Everything costs money. You need money to buy the home you have been dreaming about. It will take money as well to drive that car that you have been wanting off the lot. All the genie asked of him was to make a wish. The genie's job was not to paint a picture of what the young man's life should look like for him. The genie understood that the young man's destiny was already inside of him. He didn't need a handout; he needed someone to challenge him—to get out of him that which was already inside of him. Everything you need, to get everywhere you need to be, is already inside of you. But without a strong desire, and I stress a strong desire, to know or learn something we will never experience the change we so desperately say we want!

Principle 6: *You have to saddle your dreams before you can ride them.*

I got so excited I sort of gave away the next point, which is my favorite. Ask—*ask for anything you desire and your wish is my command.* This principle is one of my favorite success principles because it single handedly placed me in a position of greatness. Through this principle I was able to go from rock bottom; sleeping in abandoned buildings and eating out of trashcans to making all my dreams become a reality. The thing I love most about this principle is that all it requires is a healthy imagination. You don't have to be a genius or intellectually advanced to experience change. In fact, when I began this process over 25 years ago, it was the worst academic year of my life. Remember what I shared? Change requires desire. Once you get to a place in your life where you really want change to take place, guess what? *"BOOM!"* your genie will appear and say, "Ask of me anything and your wish is my command."

And that's exactly what I did; I made a wish. I remember that day like it was yesterday. Without a dime in my pocket or a place to go, I just sat there and used my imagination. I imagined what my life would be like and what type of things I would have. And even today, I recall those moments as some of the most amazing moments of my life. In those few precious minutes I was no longer homeless. Instead, I lived in a beautiful ranch style home with a loving family, a red picket fence, and it was near a gorgeous body of water. I couldn't figure out what I was doing professionally, but in some capacity I was helping people help themselves. My life was peaceful and drama free.

With desire and imagination alone you can begin to live the life you have dreamt of living. Let me explain how the concept works. Your imagination is like a GPS system. In order for a GPS to work, you must first power it on. I don't care how basic of a model or complex your GPS system is; it does not work if you don' turn the power switch to the on position. Once you have powered it up; get ready, get ready, get ready. The only thing left to do before your GPS takes you where your heart desires, is to select a POI (Point of Interest) or provide an address. Bottom line, I used my imagination to rewrite the script of my life and began heading in a new direction.

Let's stop and do an imagination exercise I call, "Can You See What I See?" First, I want you to ask yourself a very important question. What do you want your life to look like? The operative question is what do you want? The question is not, what does your life currently look like? I am not interested in that answer because it has absolutely nothing to do with the price of tea in China.

For this exercise, I need you to focus solely on what you want your life to look like in the future. The key to this exercise is for you to use all of your creative energy on the rest of your life instead of wasting it focusing on things you cannot change. *Note: There are no guidelines or rule to this exercise; it is your life and your imagination. You have the power to be as creative as possible.* Remember, this is your life. You are the CEO, CFO, CIO and whatever other O's I might have overlooked. You are the executive director and the screenwriter of your life, so let's begin. Here are a few questions to help you start the process.

- Write your role in the movie. Who and what do you wish to be?
- What are your goals and dreams? What time frame do you have for them?
- What would your average day, week or month look like if you were living out your dreams?
- What would be your major accomplishments in 1 year, 5 years, 10 years or more?
- What type of legacy do you wish to leave behind for your family, friends, and society as a whole?
- What type of wealth will you need to accomplish all your dreams?
- What type of information or knowledge would you need to acquire to support your dream?

There are a million other questions you or I could have generated that would get our imaginations racing. The questions in and of themselves are not as important as your responses. What you envision in your mind, how you see yourself, and how you envision the world around you is of great importance because those things become your focus. They become the reason why you go to bed at 10:00 pm and wake up at 4:00 am. They become the reason why you work two jobs during the day and attend class at night. They become the reason you make the sacrifices you make. In short, the things you desire to do, to have, and to be will provide you with the passion, the purpose, and the drive you need to succeed.

This is why I say change is not complex. You can have good credit, bad credit, or NO CREDIT at all, and the change you so desperately need in your life can be as real as the sun is bright. The best part of it all is that you do not need a cosigner for change. I don't care what people say about your breakthrough or what they think about your breakthrough. The only thing you need to get your breakthrough is a strong desire. It starts with you, and it can start as soon as you are ready for it to start. You can activate the process this very moment if you have enough curiosity to ask yourself one simple question, "What would it take to get from where I am now to where I want to be?" Or you can continue to live a life of lack and be envious of those around you who are enjoying every minute of their lives. You don't need to go to a beach to find the genie in a bottle. Your change is the bottle and all you need to do is be daring enough to rub your bottle and your wishes can become your reality

Summary: Principles 4-6

- Principle 4: Learn to be curious.

- Principle 5: Don't be afraid to explore your curiosity.

- Principle 6: You have to saddle your dreams before you can ride them.

CHAPTER

6

When I Move You Move

"A year from now you may wish you had started today."
- **Karen Lamb**

I don't remember much of what I learned in middle school, especially not in science class. However, I do recall doing a lesson that elaborated on the differences between potential energy and kinetic energy. **Potential energy** is energy that is stored in an object. If you stretch a rubber band, you will give it potential energy. As the rubber band is released, potential energy is changed to motion. **Kinetic energy** is the energy of motion. A rubber band flying through the air has kinetic energy. When you are walking or running your body is exhibiting kinetic energy. **Potential energy is converted into kinetic energy.** Before the yo-yo begins its fall, it has stored energy in relation to its position. At the top, it has its maximum potential energy. As it starts to fall the potential energy begins to be changed into kinetic energy. At the bottom, its potential energy has been converted into kinetic energy causing the yo-yo to reach its maximum kinetic energy.

Based on my limited understanding of the scientific terminology used to explain this concept, my hypothesis is that desire and imagination could be classified as potential energy. Both desire and imagination are stored in the mind of the individual and when stretched, both have the potential to position a person for greatness. Individually, neither is capable of producing any real outcomes. Thus having a desire for change and dreaming about change is merely the initial stage of change.

Essentially, what distinguishes potential energy from kinetic energy is eight letters. M.O.V.E.M.E.N.T. And those eight letters that formed the word movement are the exact same entities that separate the stagnant: those who are on the treadmill of life going nowhere fast—running in circles experiencing one defeat after another—from the more progressive—those walking in their anointing; living their purpose; and experiencing victory after victory. Having potential is imperative to success, but there is a time and season for everything. You cannot afford to live in potential for the rest of your life; at some point, you have to unleash the potential and make your move(ment).

Principle 7: *Choosing friends is a matter of life and death.*

I once heard a wise man say, "If you find yourself in a hole, the worst thing you can do is keep digging." I never thought I would say this, but being homeless turned out to be a blessing. It put me in a position that forced me to rethink some things and change my perspective on life. For instance, living with my brother Tim seemed like the ideal thing to do when the thought of where I would find shelter initially popped into my head. Sometimes you have to be careful what you ask for because you just might get it. Like I said, living with him made sense at the time: it meant security, and it meant not having to worry about having a roof over my head or dealing with some of the other challenges associated with being homeless. But there was one small problem; living with Tim didn't help change my mentality or my attitude. Homelessness had the opposite effect: it didn't provide me with the luxuries I was accustomed to when I lived at home, but it sure did change my way of thinking. It lit a fire under my butt that my teachers, my counselors, and even my parents couldn't manage to ignite.

Homelessness stripped the immature, self-centered, nonchalant attitude right out of me and caused me to take life more seriously. For instance, when I was homeless I approached relationships entirely different.

Pre homelessness was all about having fun, nothing more nothing less. I chose most of my friendships based on proximity; my friends lived in the same neighborhood or went to the school that I attended. I had no real formula for choosing the people in my inner circle other than having fun. When I was homeless and didn't live in a specific neighborhood, choosing friends was an entirely different story. The days of living life like it was a video game were over. In the video game, the outcome of the gamer's decisions doesn't matter much. Whether the gamer wins or loses he can always push the restart button and the system will give him a new player and a fresh start. It didn't take me long to figure out on the street level they weren't playing any games and that there was no restart button. You pay upfront for every decision. Life was for keeps; I couldn't start over and there was little to no room for error. I had to grow up quickly. One of the ways I changed my circumstances was to think long and hard about whom I called a friend. Based on my circumstances, I knew for sure one of the qualities I was looking for in a friend was someone who could help me elevate my game. I figured out early that I could "do bad" by all by myself. I had that Kevin Garnett mentality—I wasn't looking to leave Minnesota, I was just tired of coming up short and needed desperately to surround myself with people who had that winner's mentality. I tasted my share of defeat, and I wasn't fond of the taste. I wanted to surround myself with the kind of people who could help me turn my life around; people whom I could rub up against like iron and be sharpened. So my first move toward recovery was thinking methodically about all the people whose paths I crossed that fit that description. It didn't matter if we went to elementary, middle, or high school together. It didn't matter if they were black, white, green or yellow. The only thing that mattered was digging myself out of the hole I was in. The more I thought about it, the more one name kept popping up in my head, Robert Earl King, a.k.a. Bob, B. or the R.A.W Babe which was weird because of all the people I thought about I knew Bob the least.

I met Bob a year before I moved to Southfield Lathrup. We actually went to Henry Ford High School together, but with a student population of more than 2,000 it's easy not to know all your peers. I met Bob through a mutual friend, Meechie. Meechie and the whole Pierson crew got tired of Braile Street boys spanking that tail in basketball and football every year, so Meechie violated the neighborhood rules and recruited an outsider.

The street rivalries dated back to the late 70's. Several rival streets got together during the year and played each other in sports. We called it "Street Wars." Before everyone started the violent movement of shooting and killing each other, we battled on the court and on the field. Our generation was stacked with talent. Lonzo was a year older than I was and together we were a dominant force, so I didn't trip when Bob came on the scene because he raised the level of competition and he seemed like a cool guy.

On the court, we actually hit it off well, and as luck would have it, we were assigned to the same English class the next school year. Towards the end of the school year we were just starting to develop our friendship when I moved to Lathrup. Once I moved to the burbs, our friendship ended and even though only four miles separated us, I didn't see or talk to Bob until I thought about him that day.

As I look back on my life I can say that the single most life altering move (not desire) I ever made was reconnecting with Bob. My relationship with him confirmed what my parent's had been trying to get me to understand for years. The people you associate yourself with have the greatest influence on your life. Your relationships will either make you or break you and there is no such thing as a neutral relationship. People either inspire you to greatness or pull you down in the gutter, it's that simple. No one fails alone, and no one succeeds alone.

When I reconnected with Bob I felt as fortunate as K.G. (Kevin Garnett) when he left Minnesota for Boston. I, too, moved beyond the thought of repositioning myself to actually taking the necessary steps to reposition myself and join a group of men that could help me compete for a championship. Time will not allow me to write about all the ways Bob helped me to climb from the bottom to the top, but I will share six lessons I believe are needed for those of you who are tired of hanging with scrubs and want to be in the winner's circle.

Lesson 1:   Look for people who believe in something and are passionate about their beliefs.

Contrary to popular opinion, money, position, and power are not the true measure of success—**character** is the foundation for all real success. Before I met Bob I can honestly say that I never really thought about character, but even at a young age, Bob made character look appealing. He was the only popular Christian I knew and he was one of the best rappers in our neighborhood. He was known for making dudes cry in a capping session and the ladies loved him! Most of the Christians I met in school were lame. Every word that came out of their mouths was Jesus, Jesus and Jesus, but Bob had swag. However, swag was not what drew me to Bob, what drew me to him was the fact that Bob never compromised his beliefs.   It didn't matter who we were with, or where we were, Bob stood for something and did not change his beliefs for anyone.   I admired that about him because I knew first -hand how easy it was at that age for a young man to let peer pressure break him. I met so many fake people in high school.   On Sunday they were in the front row at church, they sang in the choir, and probably taught Sunday school. They were raised in a good Christian home, but as soon as they walked out of the front door, they tried to act like somebody they were not just to be a part of the in crowd. Bob was just the opposite. I can't explain the feeling but watching someone keeping it "one-hundred percent" was empowering.

Bob made standing up for what you believed in cool and by making it cool he unknowingly empowered me. I no longer felt obligated to down play my personal beliefs in order to make other people happy. Through Bob, I learned to live out loud. I was still a virgin in high school and proud of it. Back then, if someone questioned me about it, I would lie and act like I was some type of player. Deep down inside, the thought of losing my virginity to a stranger just wasn't appealing. I wasn't a Christian, so it wasn't like I was trying to wait until marriage, I just didn't want to lose my virginity to someone I wasn't in love with. At the time, I was much more concerned about what others thought about me than I was about standing up for my personal beliefs. Bob was instrumental in helping me overcome that. He helped me understand the importance of character.

Character isn't something that happens to you. With each decision that I made, I was consciously or subconsciously forming my character. Character is like my fingerprint; it identifies me from everyone else in the world. It says who I am and where I am headed. Bob helped me realize that I had a choice and that I needed to exercise my choice.

I was famous for saying that my teachers didn't like me, but not once did I ask the question why? Why did my teachers not like me? I was always the victim, I was the one being picked on or judged by my teachers, but I never stopped to consider how the quality of my character affected how my teachers viewed and treated me. It wasn't that my teachers didn't like me or that they were picking on me, it was the messages I was conveying through my character. My mouth said I wanted to be in class and I wanted to learn, but my character was speaking so loudly, the teachers couldn't hear a word I was saying. I was reaping what I sowed. It's a simple equation—you sow apple seeds you get apple trees. Things change for the better when we take responsibility for our own thoughts, decisions, and actions.

Lesson 2: Be a giver, not a taker.

It's one thing to have a friend, it's another thing to have a friend you can trust. You could put your wallet in Bob's back pocket and he would get it back to you first thing the next morning. Beyond that, Bob would give it back to you with some money in it—he was just that kind of guy. In fact, when I first reconnected with Bob I didn't have a dime to my name, but Bob made sure I didn't want for anything. If Bob bought *Better Made* barbeque chips and a *Faygo* peach pop, I had *Better Made* chips and a *Faygo* grape pop (peach was too strong). Bob's father was murdered when he was just 8 years old. I don't know the whole story, I just heard he was an addict and he got shot over something drug related. Because of his father's death, every month Bob received a Social Security check and I swear whenever he got his check it was like I received a check. If Bob had it, it didn't make a difference what it was, I had it. When Bob bought his first car, I had a car. Whenever I needed a ride to work he either dropped me off, picked me up or he let me borrow the car. His clothes were my clothes, no strings attached. He didn't do for others, or me for that matter, with alternative motives and I believe Bob was so blessed because he was such a giver.

I remember Bob got drunk one night at a party and got into it with the wrong dudes. One of the dudes pulled out a 38, aimed it at Bob and emptied the chamber. I don't know exactly what happened that night; all I know is that Bob lived to tell the story and the only thing that got shot was the windshield of the car. Another time Bob was away for the weekend on a "run," and while he was in the house he said he noticed a cab car that looked out of place. When he told some of our homies, they dismissed it and said it was just a cab and that he was tripping, but Bob said his spirit told him something was wrong. Bob told the guys he was going to go to the corner store to get a bag of chips and a *Faygo* pop. When he got back to the spot, 15 minutes later, he saw police all over the place. He said he walked past the house and sure enough it was a full-blown raid! Bob walked right through the lights and the sirens as if he was a passerby and was never detected.

Lesson 3: Always remain loyal.

One of the things that my father stressed to me was the importance of being true to my word. He talked about a time when men didn't need contracts for every transaction, and that if a man gave his word, by looking a person in the face and shaking his hand, the agreement was as good as gold. That was Bob. Bob was true to his word and truer to our friendship.

When we first reconnected, Bob snuck me in his grandparent's house; however, Bob's older brother Bill wasn't too happy about it. When Bob's father died, his grandfather took custody of Bob and his brothers, and he built a nice size room for the boys in the basement. The room had two sets of bunk beds in it. I slept under Bob's bed on the floor—this sounds uncomfortable, but it beat sleeping outside. Bill was pissed because he looked at it this way: there were already four boys sharing one basement. After about a week he squealed and told his step grandmother whom he didn't get along with but he knew if he told gramp, gramp wouldn't put me out on the street. Bob was pissed when he found out what happened; even though Bill was his big brother, Bob's loyalty never changed. He spoke with his grandfather and let him know that he was going to let me stay in Bill's K-Car, which had recently been in an accident.

Whatever his step grandmother cooked for breakfast, lunch or dinner, Bob made sure I got a plate. In the morning he unlocked the door and let me take a hot shower. If you looked the word loyal up in the dictionary, you would probably see a picture of Bob. I learned that a real friendship is not about what you can get, but what you can give. Real friendship is about making sacrifices and investing in people to help them improve their lives.

Lesson 4: Maintain a positive outlook.

I am a firm believer that a person does good when he feels good. A lot of people like to downplay power of thinking positively and being a positive person. Being around Bob convinced me that there is real power in positivity. I don't care what the weather was or what day of the week it was, Bob kept a smile on his face and a song in his heart. No matter what the circumstances were, Bob had a positive outlook on life. Whenever I was in his presence I forgot I was homeless. I think the fact that Bob had been through his own personal struggles and managed to keep his head up and remain positive made his witness that much stronger. He wasn't some kid born with a silver spoon in his mouth, but he used the principles of positivity to get through his own struggles. Bob lived in a three-bedroom house with his four brothers, his grandparents and his stepmother, and her three daughters. His grandfather was the sole breadwinner for the household. His mother was a substance abuser and was in and out of his and his brothers' lives, but no one would have ever known that my boy, Bob, wasn't born into royalty. He walked like it, he talked like it, he carried himself like it, and he forced the people who knew and loved him to treat him like it. It was that bravado that transformed my thinking and gave me energy to keep pressing toward my goals. After being in his presence I was convinced that positive people enjoy certain luxuries; they experience deeper joy and go through less stress than pessimistic people do. Through Bob I learned to look at hardships as learning experiences and even on the most miserable day I could hold the promise that tomorrow is a new day that promises to be better.

Lesson 5: Never underestimate the power of words.

I truly believe that life and death are in the power of the tongue. I believe we have to be careful about the messages that we allow to enter our minds and the messages we convey to others because words have such power. I am a living witness that words that are spoken to you can bring forth life to your soul or death to your soul. I know this first hand because Bob's words coached me back to life. I remember Bob talking to me about some college down south called Oakwood. He was so animated and excited about it (later I found out that he had never even visited the school). He talked about how he thought it was the perfect college for me and that he thought I should go and study ministry. After Bob got me all excited, I found some literature on the school at church and began dreaming about the possibilities of going there some day.

I learned from Bob the power of words and how they can influence lives. There have been times in my life when close family members and friends spoke words that crushed me. "You are going to be just like your biological father, you'll never qualify for that or you're not smart enough to do that." Words in the hands of the wrong people can not only crush your spirit, but they can also derail your dreams, skew your self-image, and hurt your heart. Bob's words of life brought me in touch with the two most critical relationships in my life today. The first one was with my first real relationship with a female and the second was my relationship with Jesus Christ.

Lesson 6: A true friend respects your values.

Unfortunately for Bob and me, the church wasn't the only environment in which we spent quality time. As we got older we spent more of our time hanging out on Mark Twain and less time on the 7 Mile and Trinity. Even though the two were close in proximity, they were like worlds apart. Detroit in the late 80's was a weird city because one block could totally define what type of social economic status a person experienced. The houses on the deep west side of Detroit looked well manicured. They were made with beautiful red brick, had manicured lawns, and new cars in the driveway. If a person traveled further toward the east, he became more aware of the realities of poverty in an industrial powerhouse. When I use the term poverty it is much deeper than just living below the nation's poverty line. Poverty was a mindset. For the first time in my life I was fully exposed and experiencing the realities of poverty. I had family members who lived in Cabrini Green, in Chicago's housing complex, and some lived in the Herman Gardens housing complex. I spent the night at my grandmother and aunt's house on a regular basis and hung out with my cousins.

Gradually, the street values began to have a heavy influence on the two of us. Bob more so than me because Mark Twain was his old stomping ground. Eventually, Bob started drinking, smoking and hustling. I was more into the apparel game and gambling. I helped my customers purchase name brand apparel at discounted prices. I would go into the mall of their choice, find their items, steal the merchandise, and sell it for 50% off the retail value. I always appreciated that Bob did not pressure me into smoking and drinking. When the guys rolled up the Tops and began passing the joint Bob would say, "Don't pass that joint to E, ya'll know E don't smoke." Even as far as the ladies were concerned, Bob knew that I was a virgin, but he never joked on me about it or tried to convince me that I needed to change my conviction. If I wasn't feeling it, Bob never pressed the issue or used his leverage in our friendship to manipulate me.

Summary: Principle 7

- **Choosing friends is a matter of life and death.**

- Lesson 1: Look for people who believe in something and are passionate about their beliefs.

- Lesson 2: Be a giver, not a taker.

- Lesson 3: Always remain loyal.

- Lesson 4: Maintain a positive outlook.

- Lesson 5: Never underestimate the power of words.

- Lesson 6: A true friend respects your values.

CHAPTER

7

Go Where You're Celebrated
Not Tolerated

"If you associate yourself with Eagles you will learn to soar to great heights." - **Unknown**

I think I made it quite obvious why it is so important to surround yourself with the right people. Your destiny and your dynasty is determined or demolished by those closest to you. Now that we have established the need for you to take a thorough look at those you have selected in your Fave Five or your inner circle, it's time to look at the next step toward your success—your environment. Here is the question you need to ask yourself before you enter any environment, "Is this soil the ideal environment for the type of harvest I am expecting to gain?" When I was a young man, my mother had a garden that I was equally responsible for. My mother taught me several things that I needed to take into consideration before planting my seed in just any dirt. First, I needed to examine the dirt. I needed to be certain to identify the best soil type for the growth of my seed. Next, I needed to select dirt that was disease free and that contained enough nutrients to feed the seed. Those who want success should think like a planter. They should understand that having the right seed is an essential key to success, but they must also understand that the soil that they entrust to the seed is just as vital. Those who understand this concept realize that the operative word for planting is not growth—growth can and will happen in most environments. The operative word is type! In the initial season, the success seeker is not anticipating growth; instead, he should search for the proper environment for growth to take place. Can you honestly say the environment(s) you are in will yield the kind of harvest you are expecting? If not, then you might want to get in position to reposition yourself.

That's what I did over twenty years ago. I repositioned myself. One day Bob came to me and said he was going to give me an opportunity of a lifetime. He said it was only under one condition; I had to be ready to get ready. Although it was a great offer, he said he wouldn't make the proposition if I wasn't ready for it. It took me about two months to clear my head and finally make the decision to take Bob up on his offer. He offered me the opportunity to come and visit the environment that made him the person he was, his church.

I thought changing my circle of influence had improved my life. Then I was exposed to the environment that made Bob into the person he was. The crazy thing is that my growth had nothing to do with the church itself. My growth was connected to the environment the church produced. The church was only a tiny little storefront church on Puritan and Ward with less than 100 members, but sometimes looks can be deceiving; bigger is not necessarily better. The Detroit Center Church created the type of environment that could reform the most rebellious, immature, and misguided young person in the entire world. I know what you are thinking. How soon can I pack my bags, turn in my two weeks notice and relocate to the West Side of Detroit? There is no need to go to such drastic measures. I am going to share the top 4 methods the Detroit Center Church used to help reform my life and prepare me for greatness.

Principle 8: The right environment is pivotal to your success; embrace environments that positively contribute to your growth.

It hurts just thinking about that Final Four game. It was the NCAA road to the Final Four. Sixty-four teams entered the tournament and somehow they managed to survive and compete for the National Title. It was a nail biting experience, and with less than 13 seconds on the clock they were in striking distance. My team's opponent missed the free throw, the ball hit the back of the rim and my team got the rebound and headed down the court. Once they passed half court the forward dribbled the ball in the corner to set up a play and got double-teamed. With no play open and no help on the backside his instincts kicked in and he called a timeout. As he called the timeout, he realized there were no timeouts left. The ref called a technical foul and with less than 13 seconds on the clock, the other team went to the free throw line to shoot two free throws and won the game. The Fab Five stood on the court in shock as they suffered their second defeat 77 to 71 in the 1993 NCAA finals. I could see the look of disappointment on the face of Chris Weber as he walked off the court. I have never had the privilege of personally meeting Weber, Jalen Rose (whom I named my son after), or any the other members of the Fab Five, but trust me when I say I can relate to the pain Weber felt when falling short of his goal when it was only a few inches away.

Years before Weber ever stepped on the court, I was given a golden opportunity. It was the fall of 1987, on the west side of Detroit. It began like any other random church service. There were a ton of preliminaries, an A and B selection from the choir, and the pastor spoke. Everything was copasetic until the end of his message. I swear he started staring and preaching directly at me as if there were no other members in the church.

"The Lord admonishes us to forgive our debtors as He has forgiven us of our debts. Forgiveness is not a feeling, but it is a command. God is not offering you a pardon, a stay or a pass when it comes to forgiveness.", he pressed. "We must all be willing, as He has been, to forgive our neighbors. Regardless of the pain we have suffered at the hands of our enemy, no matter the offense, we must free ourselves."

He stated with a convicting voice, "I know first- hand what it's like to have an opportunity, to be so close to getting over the hump, but somehow falling short right at the end." I was listening attentively when the pastor got to the part about forgiveness—the part about freeing your enemy so you could free yourself. The way he said it struck a nerve. Forgiveness was so far in the back of my mind, and so was that incident. I hadn't thought about the incident since I left. But when he said, "In order to hold someone down, you must stay down with them." That one statement alone knocked the wind out of me. Was he suggesting that my success was somehow connected to my willingness to surrender my anger and forgive her for what she did to me?

"I am going to count down from 10 and give you an opportunity to come to the altar and respond to this appeal. And more importantly, I am giving you an opportunity to do more than forgive your enemies. I am giving you an opportunity to get your life back. By setting your enemies free, you unconsciously free yourself." I am sure no one sitting beside me could see the all out brawl, the internal war that was happening inside of me. On one hand, I wanted to put it past me so I could move on with the rest of my life, but on the other hand, I didn't want to just let her off the hook that easy. She put me through too much pain for me to just forgive her and move on. But I kept thinking to myself, *"Here is your opportunity, your chance to get that monkey off your back. All you have to do is go up there and get it off your chest."* Just as I was about to stand up and do it, I heard a voice say, *"Think about it, she hasn't forgiven you for what you've done. She never even accepted responsibility for her actions. Don't humiliate yourself."* All of a sudden, I jumped on my feet, and started walking past the individuals sitting next to me in the pews. Once I made it to the aisle, I looked at the pastor and his eyes met mine. The eye contact only lasted a split second, but it felt like hours. I turned toward the exit and ran out of the front door and on to Puritan Avenue. Bent over and clutching my knees, gasping for air with sweat dripping from every pore, I began to relive the entire event over in my head as if it were happening for the first time. I grew ten feet because of that one sermon.

In the right environment, you should get the sense that you are being celebrated and not tolerated.

If you ask me what grabbed my attention the first time I walked through the doors of Detroit Center, I would have to say it was the way the people embraced me. And I knew it was genuine because I came to church in street clothes *(at the time I didn't have the money to buy church clothes)*. But apparently it didn't matter; they were more concerned with making me feel welcomed than they were with the kind of clothes I was wearing. And even though I was impressed with the initial warm greeting, I was about to fall for the ying yang. I was only there because Bob invited me. I knew Bob was down for me like four flat tires, but there was no way in the world anyone could get me to believe that the people in that church could show me the same type of love Bob showed me. And if you asked me six months after I entered the church what made me stay—with tears running down my face, I would have to tell you—it was the love. Although I didn't have any intentions of joining Bob's church or anyone's church, I continued to attend because I understood that it would be stupid to leave a place that showed me as much love as the people at that church showed me. After the first month of attending church Sister Burse told me it was my turn to teach the youth bible class. I didn't even own a bible and she put me in the rotation. It didn't matter that I was homeless and potentially on the verge of being a high school dropout; she believed in me. The church's philosophy was, you are only a guest once, the next time you walk through those doors we are putting you to work. And boy did they put me to work. After my first major assignment, Sister Burse pulled me aside and encouraged me. She said she noticed

I had leadership potential and I should continue teaching; I guess that's why she gave me several opportunities after that day. More importantly, she took an interest in me and took the time out of her schedule to train me. Looking back on those days I can truly say that she helped me hone my speaking and leadership skills and taught me how to operate in what she called a spirit of excellence.

What was even deeper and even more impressive was the fact that The Center Church didn't just embrace me behind closed doors, they invited me to go on the church retreat and they even covered all my expenses. Their acts of kindness sent a huge message. I felt like I was a part of the family, like I belonged. It was like being on the sitcom Cheers listening to the theme song.

"Making your way in the world today
takes everything you've got.
Taking a break from all your worries
sure would help a lot.
Wouldn't you like to get away?
Sometimes you want to go
Where everybody knows your name,
and they're always glad you came.
You wanna be where you can see;
our troubles are all the same
You wanna be where everybody
knows your name."
You wanna go where people know,

> *people are all the same,*
> *You wanna go where everybody*
> *knows your name."*

In the right environment, you should feel upgraded.

No more than about thirty days after I joined the church, Sister Cash came up to me after church and asked me about my family situation. She said she overheard one of the teenagers talking and they said I didn't have a place to stay, that I was homeless. As soon as I told her I was homeless, she offered her home. And it wasn't like she was well off. She and her husband, Brother Cash, had three children, Rodney, Raymond, and Renee. No one in the house was working and they were on assistance, but she treated me like family.

Being blessed with a roof over my head was only the beginning. A few months after looking for work, finding little odd jobs here and there, I was employed at the McDonalds right up the street from the church on Fenkell and Wyoming. The pastor kept preaching about returning a faithful tithe and offering, so by faith I took him up on his offer. I was a little skeptical at first. I wasn't sure how the whole tithe and offering thing went, and I wasn't sure how the church managed my money, but my thinking changed when he read Malachi 3:16:

Test me in this," says the LORD Almighty, "and see if I will not throw open the floodgates of heaven and pour out so much blessing that there will not be room enough to store it. 11 I will prevent pests from devouring your crops, and the vines in your fields will not drop their fruit before it is ripe," says the LORD Almighty. 12 "Then all the nations will call you blessed, for yours will be a delightful land," says the LORD Almighty.

When I heard about how we should test God, I started thinking to myself I didn't have much to lose in the first place. My ten-percent was around $60.00, if that. I wasn't the smartest apple in the bunch, but if God was going to do all the pastor said he would do for $60.00, it was worth a shot. I looked at it like this, I spent $60.00 on a pair of shoes and Footlocker never promised me anything; and so many positive things had happened since I had become a part of the family, I would be a fool not to invest in the people who invested into me.

In the right environment, Big I's and little you's don't exist.

Another thing I really appreciated about Pastor Willis and the way he ran the church was the fact that he didn't tolerate pecking orders. It didn't matter if people had Dr. in front of their name, MD behind it or if they were his own flesh and blood, he created an environment where everyone could be a stakeholder. Everyone was not only allowed to make suggestions about church growth and their voice was actually heard. Meetings were not just a formality; he was really interested in what all the members had to say. It didn't matter if they were educated, uneducated, young or old, he would listen. In fact, one year we had a youth week of prayer and everyone who was willing to follow a few guidelines was allowed to make a presentation. He made his son follow the same guidelines and he divided the responsibilities between all the youth evenly.

The right environment allows you to set realistic expectations while simultaneously providing pressure.

I am not sure who ran their mouth, but word got back to Pastor Willis that I dropped out of school. Initially, he just asked me about it. Even though I was going to church regularly, I still had not been completely converted. I didn't lie to the pastor about my school status, but I was extremely evasive. He didn't say much at first, but he was a military man so I knew it wouldn't take long before he turned up the heat and treated me like I was his son. "Son," he said, "I need you to either go back to school or I need you to get your G.E.D. You have too much talent to waste your time on these streets. You are going to be something one day, so don't allow this little obstacle to stand in your way. After you get your G.E.D. I am going to see to it that you go to college. In fact, I will personally write you a letter of recommendation." I thought it was a very motivational display for a pastor. If I didn't know any better I would have thought he meant every word he said, but I was too smart for that. I knew he only said it because he was a pastor and that's what pastors do. He probably said that to every young person in his congregation. Plus, I had been told by teachers that I was a clown, and I wasn't disciplined enough to go to college. So I dismissed the thought and kept going to church like we never had the conversation. That didn't deter him much; a few weeks later in church, Sister Willis (our First Lady) came up to me and asked if I ever started working on that G.E.D. *"I can't believe pastor talked to you about that, I thought that was between the two of us?"* I thought. She gave me that, I am his wife he tells me everything look. "No ma'am, I haven't been back to school." "Go get your G.E.D. baby and go to college," she said as she gave me a big motherly hug and a soft kiss on the cheek. "I love you."

I loved the entire Center family but there were times I hated the pressure they put on me to excel and be great. But whenever I think about wanting to be in a pressure free environment, I think of this quote by Peter Marshall, *"When we long for life without difficulties, remind us that oaks grow strong in contrary winds and diamonds are made under pressure."*

CHAPTER

8

Momentum Is Promiscuous: One Day It's With You, The Next Day It's Gone...

"Promiscuous girl, Wherever you are"
"I'm all alone and it's you that I want"
"Promiscuous Boy, You already know
That I'm all yours, what are you waiting for?"
- **Nelly Furtado ft. Timbaland- Promiscuous Girl**

After a sporting event the head coach of the losing team is often asked about the game and what went wrong. The answer often begins with "we lost the momentum." It's a phrase commonly used to describe why things are not going in our favor at a particular time. The way in which we use the phrase makes it seem as if momentum is an object that we can physically touch or feel, such as "we lost the keys." The truth is that momentum, in the sense in which we are discussing, is a feeling, and if it's a feeling, that means we have the ability to have it on our side at all times if we so choose. It took me a while to figure out this concept.

I was sitting in church one day when Elder Craig walked up to the microphone and said he was going to teach the congregation how to never have another bad day in their life. I took a personal interest because it seemed as though my luck was running low. Less than four months after I started living with Sister Cash she decided she had enough of Detroit, so she moved back down south to Atlanta. Once again, I was homeless and it was starting to effect my disposition. I was slowly slipping into a depressive state. The elder grabbed the microphone, opened his bible, and read a passage from Proverbs 17:22, which states, "A merry heart does the body good like medicine." It was simple, but it made sense. That was the reason Bob was so optimistic, he understood the true meaning of the text. He knew that our disposition was related to our destiny in the same way as a steering wheel is related to a car. Your disposition controls the destination of your life and places you in a position to succeed.

Reprogramming My Mind

God knew I needed a better coping mechanism to get me through the mental anguish of being homeless. Being separated from my family and not being able to talk to my mom on a daily basis was enough to break me down mentally. The holidays were the worst. I missed being home with my family and I especially missed grandma Shirley's cooking. I knew my parents would not mind me coming over for Thanksgiving dinner or Christmas, but my pride would not let me humble myself. In my mind, calling somehow was a sign of weakness. In fact, it was that kind of thinking that made me feel like I had to cut them off—especially my mom.

It was luck that brought me to a new environment where I would be exposed to some life changing information. I learned a valuable lesson in that environment: there is power in one's spirit—the power to empower and the power to suppress. I also learned that I needed to annihilate all negative thinking. When my thoughts were consumed with negativity, the thoughts often became a self-fulfilling prophecy. Bobby McFerrin released a song that I adopted as my mantra, *"Don't Worry Be Happy."* The song had a line about being homeless that proclaimed even under those circumstances, *don't worry, be happy.* In short, the song illustrated that worrying would only further complicate the situation.

I spent a great deal of time walking and talking to myself and praying. I used my imagination to control my thoughts about what my life could be like. I sang songs. I may not have been able to carry a note, but through singing I could forget the challenges I had as long as that song was in my heart.

Once I was exposed to a new environment, it didn't take me long to discover that successful people were not successful because of some superior gene they inherited at birth. It had more to do with their outlook on life and their ability to keep momentum on their side. Through my observation of these people I discovered that I had a much better chance of placing myself in a position to succeed if I had faith. I learned that there are three categories of people when it comes to faith. The first group has no faith whatsoever. They are from Missouri, the show me state. The second group has a measure of faith, but not enough to experience any real outcomes. The last group lives by faith. They don't have to touch it, taste it, or see any evidence of it to believe they can live an abundant life. They are certain that the future is going to be full of good fortune and as a result, their expectations often become self-fulfilling prophecies.

Apply the ABC's of success to your life. Ask, Believe, and Claim it. "It doesn't hurt to Ask; the worst thing they can say is no." The only place you can go is up from there. I have upgraded to a first class seat from coach without paying any extra money on many occasions simply because

I asked. Don't let the fear of rejection keep you from experiencing next level living. After you ask, you have to Believe you are worthy enough to have whatever it is you've asked for. For years I was afraid to ask organizations and schools to pay me for speaking because I didn't believe my presentation was worthy of receiving compensation for my services, and guess what, they didn't pay me. When I finally began to believe that my presentations were worthy, the checks began rolling in. Finally, Claim it. According to the dictionary, claim means to demand as a right. In short, to claim something means to expect it long before it happens. I remember the first time I used the power of claiming it and naming it. I was looking to buy my first house and I was told that the neighborhood I wanted to live in was beyond my financial means. I had the real estate agent take me through the homes anyway and when I saw this one particular house, I knew it was mine. My realtor took me to seven other homes within my supposed budget, but I kept thinking of the one I knew belonged to me. So instead of worrying and allowing doubt to consume my thoughts, I went to the grocery store and picked up some empty boxes and started packing as if the house was already mine. A month later my realtor called and said the couple that owned the house was relocating and wanted to accept my offer. The Bible tells us, "Now faith is confidence in what we hope for and assurance about what we do not see."

Principle 9: Individuals who are able to maintain momentum listen to their intuition.

I can't put it into words, and I am not sure how I feel about the whole love at first sight concept. All I know is that whenever I was in the same room with her, I couldn't stop staring at her. It was weird because I didn't visit the church with the intent of trying to find someone to date. I was going through so much in my life that dating was the last thing on my mind. I was hoping that if I gave it a few weeks the feelings for her would pass, but something in my gut kept telling me I needed to get to know her. She had such a nurturing and caring spirit for someone so young. It took me a long time to introduce myself to her because of her mother. She reminded me of one of those secret service men who work in the White House protecting the President.

In addition to being scared of her mom, I was never the most suave guy when it came to the ladies. I never dated in middle school, and in high school I was never in a real relationship. After the first few weeks of attending church, I knew I had to take a chance. There was one problem, I didn't know if she was dating someone or if she was allowed to date for that matter. I decided to hire Bob as my personal private investigator. His job was to find out every bit of information possible without letting it be known that I was the one who needed the intel. Weeks later Bob's investigation was complete. She was single. I learned once that the Romans considered Cupid to be the god of erotic love. While I was never a believer of Roman or Greek mythology myself, there was something mythical about my emerging romance with De. I grew to love her in a way that I've only seen articulated in fairytales. My relationship with her would prove to be a huge swing of positive momentum. She was more than a girlfriend; she was my best friend. She was constantly looking out for me. Whether it meant giving me her allowance so I could have some money to eat or sneaking me into the house in the winter to sleep in her closet when I was between living situations, De had my back and never let me down. She was my angel sent straight from the Lord himself.

Principle 10: *Stop sabotaging yourself.*

While my love for De was growing exponentially, if there was one thing about her that bothered me, it was her mouth. She never held anything back. If she thought it, she said it. "I don't know why you hanging out on Mark Twain so much. You need to make up your mind what you want to do. Are you trying to get your life together for real, or are you just saying that to impress me? You know you are going to end up going to jail or get killed. I am not visiting you in jail Eric. Eric, are you listening to me?" God knows that girl was the love of my life, but I promise it didn't seem like she had a sensitive bone in her body once we started dating. She was constantly nagging me about school. I used to think Pastor Willis put her up to pushing me into getting my G.E.D. Pastor Willis knew I had a soft spot for De and that I was bound to go take my test just off the strength of the love I had for her. Whenever I think about how much De harassed me about getting my life together, I always think about the relationship between Coach Larry Brown and the Detroit Pistons. Starting point guard, Chauncey Billups, appeared on ESPN's Hot Seat the season after Larry Brown was fired. He was asked which coach the players liked most, their former coach, Larry Brown, or their new coach, Flip Saunders (keep in mind Larry Brown had won a championship with the team just a few years prior). Chauncey gave a diplomatic answer; he said the verdict was still out. But the rumor was that Flip Saunders was more of a player's coach and the guys couldn't stand Larry Brown's "no nonsense" style of leadership. Brown's philosophy was that defense wins the game, not offense. Flip Saunders gave them more freedom on defense and allowed them to open it up on the offensive end. In short, the players may have liked Flip Saunders more for his laid back style, but they never won a championship. I felt the same way about my relationship with De. I felt like she pushed me too hard. It was as if she had forgotten about all my hardships and the struggles I was going through. But De wanted us to be champions. She said, "You are sabotaging yourself hanging on the block. One minute you are in church praising the Lord and the next minute you're hanging around drug dealers and thugs. As far as I know you're selling drugs, you're out in the streets an awful lot. It's time to get serious Eric, I'm not playing anymore." I wouldn't admit it then, but she was right. De was pushing me towards greatness but I was scared to make a whole hearted attempt to reach it. I was purposely sabotaging my chances of succeeding and the momentum I had gained was quickly fading.

CHAPTER

9

Enough is Enough

You will not experience all life has to offer you or begin to experience life at its fullest as long as you are satisfied with mediocrity. You have to be disgusted with your current circumstances before your circumstances can change.

You have to be smart enough to know when life presents you with a golden opportunity and you have to be courageous enough to take advantage of it. My relationship with De was that golden opportunity, but the pressure was mounting. My mother used to say there are two types of pressure- good and bad. Mom used to put it like this, "Pressure busts pipes, but it can also make a diamond. You're a diamond." Before De and I hooked up, the only pressure I experienced was the pressure to smoke weed, join a gang, sell drugs, and to lose my virginity to an absolute stranger.

"Eric, we need to talk," De said in her I mean business voice.

"All right, but let me kiss that neck first. I haven't seen my Boo in days," I said, going in for the kiss.

"Stop playing, you play too much, you can't be serious about anything can you?" she scolded.

"Well, let me hold your hand at least." I knew she was serious because her top lip curled up. I grabbed her hand and sat her down on the top stair of the porch. "Holla at me Boo; you have my undivided attention."

"Do you love me, Eric?" she asked.

"What? Do I love you?" I asked, a little hurt. "What kind of question is that?"

"Do you?", she asked again with this weird look on her face.

"Yes, I love you."

"Well, I met with my school counselor today and she told me that I have enough credits to graduate on time."

"Wow, Boo, I am proud of you." (The fact that I had recently dropped out made her graduation even sweeter). "For real Boo I am proud of you."

"Are you really?" she said in a way that sounded like a question but it really wasn't..

"What's that all about?" I asked, a little confused.

"It's about our future. I am going to college, Eric I am not going to stay in State; I am going down south and I want you to come with me.

You want me to come?" "You and I both know that's not possible!"

"It is possible; all you have to do is go get your G.E.D. You think I don't know Pastor Willis told you if you get your G.E.D. he would talk to one of his friends in the admissions department and see if he could get you in?" Immediately, my neck started to twitch—it was a natural reaction every time I got nervous. "I don't know De. I don't know."

"I thought you said you loved me? Do you or don't you?" she tested.

"What does me loving you have to do with you going to college? Hell, this is the first time you even mentioned the fact that you were going to college. What am I supposed to do? Just because you are going to college I am supposed to pack up my life here and follow you down south?" "Eric, what life? You didn't finish school, you don't have a real job; what life are you referring to—I thought I was your life? Let me put it like this, I am leaving for college in August, and I don't plan on having a long distance relationship. So either we go together and continue our relationship or else."

Principle 11: Just Do It.

If you keep doing what you've always done, you'll keep getting what you always gotten. There will never be a perfect time or perfect situation in our life to do something we should have done a long time ago. At some point we have to stop making excuses and like Nike…Just do it.

The dare De confronted me with wasn't the first. Like I said before, when you grow up in the hood, "I dare you" is an everyday expression. However, De's dare was a different kind of beast. Accepting the challenge meant more than running up to another black male and blindsiding him, or stepping to a female and randomly asking her for her number. This dare would require more than a few minutes of my time and some random act of foolishness…no, this dare would require that I make some serious changes.

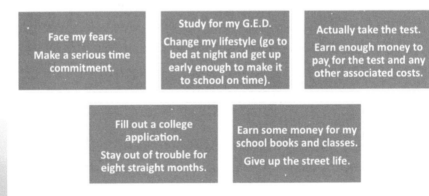

This is where most people drown, quit the race, and abandon their dreams. This is where the rubber meets the road. It is the point where the boys and the men are separated.

In retrospect, it made sense why she started the whole

conversation with, "Eric, do you love me?" "Of course I love you boo." "Then why won't you get serious about our future together?" In the short time we dated, she came to know a few things about me. One, I had absolutely no interest in school. Two, she knew it would be hard pressed for me to up and leave Bob, and she also knew it was going to be equally challenging for me to walk away from the block. She also knew that the church had a major impact on changing my life, but somehow it did not have the power to penetrate all aspects of my life. Her last chance of convincing me to take school serious was to use her influence on me.

I played it off as if I wasn't fazed, but her words hit home. I knew De cared for me, but to hear her say to my face how much I meant to her blew me away. And I knew how much I loved her, and I was willing to do whatever it took to prove my love. Wanting to prove my love and actually passing the G.E.D. were two different things. Talk is cheap; actually walking the walk requires Blood, Sweat and Tears. If I passed the test, I could leave the D, start all over again, and take my relationship with De to another level.

I will be your Motivation.

In some cases, Success is less about hard work, resources, and skill, and more about motivation. Sometimes you have to find the right incentives that push you and drive you before you can reach your dreams.

By the time I was 18 I had screwed up so much that I

started doubting myself and started believing all the venom people were spiting. The worst part was that it seemed like my mother was one of my biggest haters. She was so disappointed in my previous actions that she did not even get excited when I told her I was going to college. I guess I cried wolf one too many times for her to believe that this one was legitimate. I think she cut me off emotionally when I was about 14, because I remember her smacking me in my face and screaming, "You are going to be just like your father!" That was the first time I had ever heard her mention his name. Well, she did not actually say his name, but I knew exactly to whom she was referring. Even though she did not explain what she meant by, "You are going to be just like your daddy," I knew it was not meant as a compliment.

Then there was De De's mother, Glenda. Her hatred for me was unparalleled! In her eyes I was another thug with no future and nothing but trouble for her little princess... I wasn't mad at them though, they were entitled to their opinion, but I was on a mission to prove my mother, her mother, and the rest of my haters wrong.

No teacher, counselor, not even my parents could get me to see the value of school. Somehow De was the only one who could convince me that school was my ticket out of Detroit. Even though I was afraid I would fail and I was petrified of going to college and leaving the D, I was not going to let that stop me from keeping my word to De. I promised her that when she started school in the fall, she would not be there alone. We were going to school together and if I had it my way, we were going to spend the rest of our lives together.

When you make a decision to change, the Universe will do all in its power to make sure you have everything you need to make that change. All you have to do is be cooperative.

One evening at Wednesday night prayer service I made a deal with God. I was not sure if that was an appropriate thing to do, but I was desperate. I told God if he blessed my living situation, I would do whatever He asked me to do. No sooner than church ended, Brother and Sister Cannonier called me to the side. I was petrified, "What did I do this time?" I was so accustomed to getting in trouble that whenever an adult called my name, I knew it wasn't good. "We understand you are studying for your G.E.D. and you are planning to go to college," Sis Cannonier inquired. "Yes ma'am, those are my plans." "We have a proposal for you," Brother Cannonier chimed in. "We will allow you to move in with our family under one condition—by the end of August you have to move." They hoped by then I would be packed and ready to go to college. They made it very clear, "our home is your home as long as you are studying for your G.E.D. and pursuing college." Brother and Sister Cannonier, like the majority of the church family, had a passion for youth. I later discovered that Sister Cannoier was from Trinidad and Brother Cannonier was from

Tobago, a small island off the Atlantic Coast and like most underprivileged nations, opportunities for prosperity are scarce. They constantly reminded me of the opportunity I had as an American and how I need not take it for granted.

They did not just talk about it; they lived it. I watched them both rise early in the morning and start the day off with Worship. The house rule was that anyone who stayed the night also rose for worship. It was crazy being exposed to the West Indian grind. Sister Cannonier woke up every morning and made fresh biscuits from scratch. After she cooked, she got dressed and headed to Murray Wright High School to put in eight hours as a math teacher. Brother Cannonier was a carpenter by trade, but he had about three jobs. I am not sure which one he went to first thing in the morning, but I knew for sure he was working on one of his properties at night. He'd come home for dinner and worship then spend some time with the family before heading back out the door to work on the rental property or the church.

I was exposed to a great deal in the short time I lived with them and as a result, I learned a great deal. Of the many values I learned from the Cannoniers, the one that stuck most was the non-negotiable family worship session every morning and evening. I am not sure if their sons, Sammy and Shane, were feeling family worship, but Brother and Sister Cannonier were committed to it. They also were committed to happiness. I'm not saying they didn't have their challenges, but I saw first -hand how their faith allowed them to deal with and enjoy life in a way that was special. Hard work was another value I was exposed to. I grew up in a working class environment. I saw my parents and most of the neighbors get up in the morning and go to work, but this was a different type of work. The Cannonier's were from the West Indies, so work was a major part of their cultural beliefs. They literally gave up everything and came to the United States to create a better life for their family. Thankfully, that work ethic eventually rubbed off on me.

Principle 12: *You need your undivided attention.*

Whenever you decide to change your life for the better, just know it won't be a simple process. There will be a number of distractions enticing you to go back to your past ways.

"E, let me holla at you fam," Lil B called out. It must have been around 2 o'clock in the morning. I assumed Lil B wanted to talk about the beat down we just put on these church boys. It was something like a showdown from an old western. It started about a year ago and climaxed that night at a church basketball game. Bob, Desrick, and I were walking up a dirt road chillin' at camp meeting when we heard bass booming from a car. By the time we turned around we saw about four cats in a sports car swiftly approaching us. Instead of moving to the side and letting them pass through, I noticed B stop abruptly in the middle of the road and had this look like, I am not moving and you better slow down and go around me or something real is going to pop off up in here. Desreck and I were going to get out of the middle of the road until we noticed that B had not moved. At that point, we had to just follow B's lead. "Get out of the street before you get ran over," one of the passengers yelled. B did not blink and he did not say a word. Being out numbered was nothing new for us. In the city we would stare another brother down in a minute and dare them to fight because our crew was so massive. Plus, B's older brother Bill was there and Bill Blast was into that ultimate fighting stuff and known for giving out beat downs. Because we were outnumbered, they confidently jumped out the car to see if we would back down. After about 15 minutes of going back and forth, B said something about his older brother that was enough to shut the arguing down. Apparently, they attended the same school with his older brother and knew he had a reputation of laying cats out. As we were walking away, B let one of them know it was not over and that they better watch their backs and get ready for a serious beat down when we got back to Detroit. B kept his word. Before the fight at the game a few of us decided to go to a major church collaboration and we kind of figured they were not going to come on our side of town (the west side), but we were wrong. On my way to the restroom I noticed about three of them walking toward me, so I did a serious 180 degree rotation and ran back to the balcony and warned the guys. By the time we exited the church and dashed to the parking lot and back to the ride, they were on our trail quickly. Goodloe told us to start the car, pop the trunk, and meet him at the spot. I figured it did not take all of us to start the car, so I stayed with Loe. He was about 6 feet 4 or 5 with a long reach. As soon as the fight reached us, Loe dropped the boulders. The first dude fell back. The second one ran up on Loe and Loe landed a serious blow to his jaw that buckled him like Thomas "The Hitman" Hearns against Sugar Ray Leonard. We hopped in the ride and headed back to the Twain to holler at the rest of the crew about the near beat down and figure out how and when we were going to deal with them. B suggested we wait and surprise them. He told us they played in the church basketball league and specifically, they played against their team twice during the season and we could bum rush them in the middle of the game. B got almost everybody to commit, Sweetdaddy, BoBo, Raymond, Tank, Jr., Loe, Bill, Bob, Lil B, Descrick and without thinking I said, "I'm in." It rolled off my tongued like rain rolls off a window seal. Somehow I was in the moment and I forgot all about De and college. In that moment I felt trapped, like there was no way out. On the one hand, I wanted to sit this one out. I was a few months away from getting out of the hood and spending the next four years with my girl without her mother all in our business. On the other hand, I wanted to show my loyalty to my homies. This was my moment to show the homies my appreciation for having my back and practically raising me as far as the street game was concerned. I felt like I did not have a choice, I needed to hop in the ride and represent. One night, one ride, could change the rest of my life for the rest of my life. I guess that's why I was so grateful when Lil B called my name that night. It meant we all made it back to the block alive without anyone getting hurt or put in a bag. Plus, we made it off the premises before the police made it to the game. "E, you still headed down south for school with De in the fall?" Lil B said like a concerned parent. "No doubt," I said without being cocky but with a proud feeling. Lil B's next words shocked me because I assumed he wanted to talk about how I got down that night. "Then you need to get outta here. You are not like the rest of us, you got a chance so don't mess it up. You have an opportunity the rest of us don't' have. Get out while you are alive. I am proud of you boy, now go make the Twain proud." As I walked off the block for the last time, I turned to B and said, "I promise, college won't change me homie." I walked away from the Twain that day and I never looked back.

Got my G.E.D

At some point in life you have to face your fears, and head on even though you can't be sure of the outcome. A great deal of people will never reach their dreams and it won't have anything to do with their ability or skill set. They won't reach their dreams because they were too afraid to try.

As I took my seat, my palms were sweaty and I could feel my legs shaking uncontrollably. "E, relax, calm down, take your time, everything is going to be fine." But as soon as I closed my eyes to pray, thoughts of failure raced through my head. It was hard to ignore the negative voices screaming in my head, "It's no way you are going to pass this test, you have never been good at taking tests, you are too dumb for college," no matter how hard I tried, I could not shake the voices. Instead of panicking, I stopped and whispered a silent prayer. I remember my past experiences, that whenever I was in a crisis, if I closed my eyes, BAM! God would come through for me and I felt in my heart He could come through again. *"Though I walk through the valley of the shadow of death, I shall fear no evil for thou art with me, thy rod and staff shall protect me."* As soon as the words were leaving my lips I could feel a presence of calmness come over me, and I felt at ease. It was as if God himself came into the classroom and said in a still small voice, "Relax, take your time, everything is going to be fine son." I was young, but I was wise enough to know that if God said it, that settled it. So I grabbed my pencil, filled out my name on the Scan-tron and went to work. I approached the G.E.D. test in a way I had never approached a test. This exam had major lifelong implications. It was much deeper than an alphabetic scale, A…B…C…D or F; this exam was for all the marbles. If I failed, I knew I would be broken.

My entire future was riding on the results of this exam. For one, I could potentially lose my girl for life. Two, I would be trapped in Detroit for the rest of my life. I learned quickly that the hood is a dead end. I did not know one drug dealer that retired from the game. Even if the Feds did not catch up with them, some jealous snitch ratted them out, or some scorned female set them up. And worse than that, I did not want to be one of those cats sitting on the porch drinking a 40 oz. reminiscing about what I could have been like. On the other hand, if I passed, it was an automatic renewal on life. A renewal I so desperately needed.

The test was timed so I had to be strategic. I did not want to rush it and risk making stupid mistakes, but I could not afford to be too methodical and waste so much time focusing on one section. So my strategy was to skip all the questions I did not know immediately, and focus my energy on the questions I knew or thought I knew. The majority of the sections lasted about an hour and a half. That gave me enough time to nail the ones I knew and wrestle with the questions that were written in seemingly a foreign language. During my breaks, I was so nervous I did not speak to anyone. I did not even use the payphone to call De. I spent the entire break praying. I felt really good about my chances to pass the exam until the instructor handed out the writing portion. That's when my heart dropped. In my mind the other sections of the test were easier because they only required deductive reasoning. I read a passage and based on the information provided, I selected one of four possible answers. The writing portion was just the opposite. It was a blank sheet of paper with nothing on it. To make matters even worse, they allotted the least amount of time to complete this section. I wasted the first 15 minutes trying to create a thesis. I began writing for what seemed like five minutes, and then I heard, "Please, place you pencils down and pass your exam to the front of the room." The words pierced through my chest and I felt like I was having a massive heart attack. I closed my eyes and shook my head. I barely finished the conclusion and did not have time to edit my work. I vividly remember thinking "I got that close to having a fresh start."

"Your results will be ready tomorrow afternoon. All you need to do is visit the administrative office tomorrow after 3:00 p.m., with a valid ID and your results will be provided. However, your written portion will be mailed to D.C. for review and the results should be available within two to three weeks." "Two to three weeks!" I shouted rudely. "Yes, two to three weeks Mr. Thomas," the instructor responded. The next day I woke up with a serious knot in my stomach and I was quiet the entire day. I did not have much of an appetite, and I did not feel like being sociable. The test results were the only thing on my mind. I was dressed, out of the house, and at the bus stop one hour early. I made it to the school by 2.30 p.m. and was the first person in the office. I walked up to the window and wrote down my name, time of arrival, and my ID number. About 27 minutes later the receptionist called my name and handed me a manila envelope with my name on the top left corner and said, "Good Luck." I am generally cordial, but I was so nervous I just grabbed the manila envelope and walked out. I went outside to open the envelope so no one in the room would see my reaction to the scores. I must have walked at least a mile up the street before I opened the envelope thinking to myself, "My life is contained in this small envelope." I finally opened it and browsed through the scores. Initially, the numbers did not make a lot of sense, but at the bottom of the G.E.D. document there was a section that said you needed at least a 410 in each section and a 450 average, which would equate to 2110 points. I took a deep breath, looked down at my scores and did the mental math. I did not score a 450 in every section but when I added up all the section, I realized I passed with flying colors. Unfortunately, I had mixed emotions. I wanted to run to the nearest payphone and call De, but the last thing I wanted to do was call her and celebrate prematurely only to later find out that I failed the writing portion. In fact, I was more terrified after realizing I passed the first phase than I was taking the test in the first place. I remember thinking I had more to lose now than ever. If I had never taken the test I could always say I would have passed it if I had I taken it, I just did not feel like taking it. That way I would never have to face my fears and I could create this illusion in my mind to prevent me from feeling like a failure. I was good at that. But the stakes were high and there was no turning back at that point. If I failed the written portion, Eric Thomas

Is a Complete Failure, would be written in stone forever and my fate would be sealed. So when I finally spoke with De later that day I just told her I had to wait two weeks to get my results. It seemed like the longest two to three weeks of my life, but one random weekday I got a letter from the Department of Education. I remember sitting there looking at it for a while before I opened it. It was pouring rain outside and the wind was whipping against the window in a fierce manner. My eyes began to water and my neck began its infamous twitch. I opened the letter and read slowly. Dear Mr. Thomas the nature of this letter is to inform you that you have successfully completed the written portion of the G.E.D., congratulations. I dropped the letter and took off running down the street in the middle of the rain yelling and screaming uncontrollably. Whoo! Whoo! I ran back inside and grabbed the letter, stuck it in my pocket so it would not get wet, jumped on De's Honda Spree motorcycle and headed to her to tell her the good news. Riding through the rain with the biggest grin on my face, the only thought on my mind was, "Lookout world, here comes your boy, ET!"

It's so hard to say goodbye

Going to the next level is not as easy as one may think. People think the only requirement is giving up all the bad habits. That is the easy part. The difficult part about pursuing your dreams is that it often requires us to sacrifice some of the things we cherish. For instance, you may have

107

to sever certain relationships, certain things and certain places. It was the latter that made it so hard for me to say goodbye.

Despite all the negativity and all the things I had been through, Detroit still had a special place in my heart. Hell, all I ever really knew was Detroit so even though I was excited about the idea of going away to college, I was afraid of going so far away from home. Alabama was approximately 700 miles from Detroit—a long way from the only place I ever really knew as home. Although my mom and I had an estranged relationship and things were far from what they once were, I still thought about her and my sisters a lot and I couldn't imagine being so far from them. I did not have any family in Huntsville, Alabama or friends for that matter. I knew Alabama would not be like Detroit. I heard about the racism, the KKK, and how African Americans were treated like second-class citizens. But I was willing to take my chances and venture out in the unknown if it meant being with De.

I'll never forget the day we packed De's mother's Excursion van. After packing my bags, I had prayer with the Cannonier's. Sister Cannonier gave me a great big hug and a bag with lunch for the road. Brother Cannonier gave me a hug and said in his West Indies accent, "I am proud of you, but don't come back without your degree." Then I made my final visits. I drove by St. Bede on 12 mile, and then passed Southfield Lathrup on the way toward my parents.

As I approached the house the events that occurred over two years ago replayed in my head. As I walked through the doors, I gave my little sisters Jeneco and Malori a hug and a kiss and told them I love them and that I would miss them. I spoke with my parents briefly. They gave me a brief pep talk and $1,000.00 in cash and wished me well.

Before I went to De's house there was one more stop I knew I had to make, a stop that I had been dreading since the day I found out that I passed the test. That stop was to Bob's house. As I got out of the car I began feeling sick to my stomach. Bob meant the world to me and now I felt as if I was leaving him high and dry. On the walk up to the house I began imagining that he was coming with me and that I was just there to pick him up. I knocked on the door and Bob came out with that classic smile on his face. "You outta here boy?" he asked in an excited tone. "Yeah bro I'm out." Bob could see the anguish in my face and tried to lighten the mood. "You know I'm going to be coming down there to visit you like once or twice a month right?" "I'm getting a car soon so I am going to be down there like all the time." I remember feeling so guilty. I mean, here was the guy that poured so much into me at a time when I had nothing and nobody, and I was the one off to college while he stayed in Detroit. Bob was the first one who told me about Oakwood years ago before I even thought about college. I would have traded spots with Bob that instant if I thought I could. "Oh you're getting a ride?" was all I could manage to say. "You better get going bro, I know how De be on your head about being on time" he said laughing. "Thanks man" I said quietly. "Man you ain't gotta thank..." "Bob" I said cutting him off, "For real man, thank you for everything you've done for me." Realizing I was serious Bob reached and we executed our patented handshake we made up years ago followed by a brief hug. "Call me as soon as you get there" Bob yelled out as I opened the car door. "No doubt bro!" I yelled back. I shut the car door and headed to De's house trying unsuccessfully to hold back the tears as I rounded the corner.

On my way to De's house I drove past Henry Ford and up Trojan to Brail reminiscing the entire time. When I finally made it there, her mom had packed all De's stuff so I put my bike and my suitcase in the van and sat quietly as we headed for Alabama. We hit 75 south towards Toledo and passed Tiger Stadium. "Goodbye Detroit."

SECTION
III
THE SECRET TO
MY SUCCESS

CHAPTER

10

Oakwood: It's a Different World

"Surround yourself with positive people and look for people who are already where you want to be."

I will be the first to admit that I did not go to college with the best game plan in mind. I could not decide what I wanted to major in, and I was not really sure what courses I should or (maybe more importantly) should not take. I was like a deer in headlights. Despite my academic indecisiveness, one thing was for sure, I came too far to fail. I promised myself this time that I would choose my inner circle wisely. Like I said, I knew from first-hand experience, not from what I read in a book or from what my parents told me, how one friendship could make or break a person. So I spent the first few weeks observing. I knew I was not the smartest apple in the bunch, but my ability to judge a person's character was reliable. Those who have spent any time in the hood had to acquire this skill to survive. So like a hawk that hovers over a particular area waiting for the right moment to swoop in, I observed everybody I came in contact with. I watched and I listened to their conversations and to the best of my ability, I tried to determine who was just talking and who was serious. I knew if I were going to make it in my new environment, I would have to surround myself with individuals who knew where they were headed and had a serious plan of action. For example, I could not hook up with people because they were from Chicago or Detroit or because football was their favorite sport or because we were Virgos. If I was going to survive and get the most out of my college experience, I needed to be as strategic in selecting my inner circle as professional sports teams are with selecting players in the Draft.

With his first pick in the '89 inner circle draft, Eric Thomas selects Irvin Daphnis. What drew me to Daphnis? Like all the greats, he had an aura about him. He stood about six feet tall, he was dark with a thin build and glided across campus with this silent confidence that screamed, "Look out world 'cause here I come." Irvin was the only person I knew who was confident enough and proud enough to sport dashikis like they were Jordans. I can still picture him walking through campus with this one colorful dashiki with the continent of Africa embroidered on it. Besides his iridescent swag, Irvin was extremely intelligent but it

113

wasn't necessarily his intellect that drew me to him; it was his crossover ability that intrigued me. Even though Irv had the ability to go toe-to-toe with the best of them and although as a freshman he easily matched the intelligence of most upper classmen, he never felt the need to isolate himself from the average Joe like myself. He also had a passion for knowledge and he identified with the struggle of his people. In the words of James Brown, Irv was "Black and Proud" and did not mind saying it loud. In fact, Irv was so proud of his heritage that we nicknamed him Black.

I remember the first oratorical contest I attended and watched Irv go to work. He breezed through the first few rounds and made it to the finals. I have to be honest, I was nervous when I found out he was competing against this other freshmen by the name of Furman Fordham, also known as Pucky. I was blown away the first time I heard him speak too. His gift was his command of words; he was like a walking dictionary. We ran in different circles, but I admired him from a far. He was one of those guys who made me feel like I did not stand a chance at the collegiate level. He reminded me of one of those "most likely to succeed" guys and every time I heard him address the crowd, I kept thinking to myself, if those are the type of skills you need to succeed in college, I don't stand a chance. To my surprise, the contest was a dogfight. They went back and forth and back and forth. Pucky was doing his usual verbal acrobatics while Irv orchestrated a well-balanced speech arrayed with verbal, theatrical and contemplative skills. It was a tough decision for the judges, but to my surprise Irv pulled off the upset. I walked away from that contest a changed man. Watching another black male freely articulate in the way Irv did that day gave me the confidence that I needed to start believing in myself and my abilities. Not to mention the fact I discovered that Irv was Haitian and the fact that he was a first generation American inspired me even further. I knew if Irv's people could come to this country and succeed and help him overcome his obstacles to become the person he was, there was no excuse for me. Irv had the blue print; the competitive advantage and I needed to sit under his feet so I could learn from him.

Bell Tower Ministry

"Start where you are with what you have... what you have is plenty."

Science was not my favorite subject in school and I think that had a lot to do with the fact that it was so complex. I remember thinking there are quite a few theories to memorize and after about twenty or more I kind of figured, this might not be the subject I want to spend the rest of my life studying. But I must admit, I somewhat liked the whole symbiosis lesson because I could use it to gauge any relationship. It was simple and straight to the point. All relationships, whether the relationship was between you and your boys or with a female, fell into one of three categories.

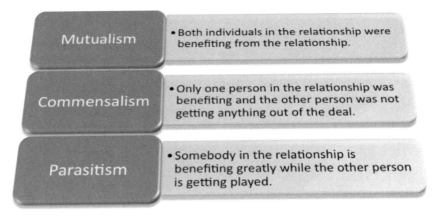

When I got to college I used the concepts from symbiosis to decide which relationship to invest in and which ones to cut. My relationship with Irv (Black) was a no brainer. I knew I was not on his level. He clearly had more to offer in the relationship then I did. For one, he finished high school and was clearly more intelligent than I was. Two, he had some leadership experience because he served as a youth leader for the Urban League in his community. And to top it off, he had impeccable administrative skills. My only challenge was to make sure I did not fall into either the commensalism or parasitism category. I knew it was not about equal giving; it was about equal sacrifice. I had a slight competitive edge because I knew what most people did not know; even the great ones need a competent sidekick. From time-to-time Batman needed Robin, the Long Ranger needed Tonto and Lavern needed Shirley. So between the codes of ethics I learned in the hood and what I knew about mutualism, I knew this relationship could create a dynamic duo.

Stay in Your Lane – Don't try to do more than you are capable of doing.

I could not have written the script any better. Three months into the school year, Black and Tre (Melvin Hadden III) called me in on an executive meeting. To this day I am not sure how Tre became a part of the team but just know Tre elevated Black and me from a dynamic duo to a tenacious trio. They wanted to let me know they felt God was leading us to do something big on campus, but they did not know exactly what it was. So Tre initiated a fast. He believed that fasting was a way of clearing the mind from all distractions so we could get in tune with the mind of God. So the plan was to fast from everything but water for seven days. I don't think I ever mentioned it to either of them but I was scared to death. I did not grow up in church, so fasting was a foreign concept. It wasn't that I did not understand the premise behind fasting; my problem was I could not understand why someone would deliberately want to go without eating for seven days. Why would anyone voluntarily inflict that type of pain upon himself (or herself); it didn't make sense to me—especially since I had already been homeless and starving on the streets of Detroit just a year prior. Despite how ludicrous the idea sounded at first, I consented. And all I can say is that three months after the fast we became a part of a groundbreaking, life-changing program that not only took the campus by storm but would also eventually transform our lives and impact the world. It was amazing to see what was birthed from a small meeting of three and a seven-day fast. The student lead initiative would be known as the Bell Tower Ministry. The concept itself wasn't new; we just took a familiar idea and added a few components to enhance it. Black was the president and founder, Tre was the vice president and our spiritual advisor, and I was the glue guy who kept us all together. By the grace of God, I was never jealous of the relationship between Black and Tre. I never once thought I should be the vice president because I knew Black first. Besides I knew Tre was a better number two man than I was and that I could best serve the squad from a supporting role. Honestly speaking, Tre's presence took us to a new level. He was so different from Black in that he added a spiritual and meek dimension that was missing. Tre was way more levelheaded and methodical than Black and I, who tended to be a bit more radical and loud. Even though my contributions were less noticeable, they were still critical to our ministry's growth.

I brought that Detroit blue-collar mentality to the squad. I helped design programs on and off campus that helped individuals regain their hope academically and spiritually. My messages were real, relevant, and delivered in plain

English. But one of the things I made sure not to do was try to duplicate what Black and Tre were doing. As long as I stayed in my lane and did not try to be a big shot, I was safe. So I passed out flyers, went from dorm to dorm announcing the event, and I also opened and closed the event with a short speech. Whatever grunt work Black or Tre asked me to do; it was an honor. As I matured, Black and Tre gradually began to give me more responsibilities and opportunities. It was a perfect demonstration of teamwork and everyone playing their position.

"I much prefer the sharpest criticism of a single intelligent man to the thoughtless approval of the masses."
- **Johann Kepler**

In addition to our weekly planning meetings, we also met weekly for what was known as Lemon Squeezes. Every Friday afternoon the executive team was required to participate in a weekly constructive criticism session. The purpose of the session was to help the members of Bell Tower Ministries identify and eliminate personal weaknesses and build on their strengths. Black always preached, "We are only as strong as our weakest link." He believed that all the great empires fell from the inside. I remember going to every meeting tense with knots in my stomach. You never knew what another one of your peers was going to say to you or someone else. The Lemon Squeeze sessions in my opinion were always dangerous. Personally, I had never been in a setting with my peers where we spoke so freely and honestly about other people's flaws. Where I was from, if a person talked about someone like that, it was bound to turn into a knockdown, drag out fight. The only time anyone remotely addressed a brother's weakness and it not turn into a fight was during a roasting session (playing the dozens). Even then if the person was not careful, it could go from a roast to a heavy weight prizefight. The rules were simple. The group would select one individual from the team to take 5 to 10 minutes sharing with a certain individual their opinion about what that person needed to work on over the next week. The team member who was critiqued was not allowed to rebut. After each member gave his remarks, the individual was then asked to explain how he could use the constructive criticism to elevate his personal and organizational game. The sessions always ended with group praise. Black believed the session should always end with the message that each individual was valued as a person and that all contributions to the organization were valued (hence the name Lemon Squeeze.) Our meetings started with constructive criticism (the individual getting squeezed) and ended with praise (adding the sugar to make lemonade). I am not sure which was more salient, the actual process or the things I learned about myself during each session. The process taught me the value of being proactive. Black realized he did not want to wait for personality differences or petty misunderstandings to erode our mission. He could cut it off before it gained any momentum. More importantly, I learned through the process that by decreasing your threats you simultaneously increase your growth and success.

CHAPTER
11

You should have put a ring on it.

"One half of me is yours, the other half yours-
Mine own, I would say; but if mine, then yours,
And so all yours!" - **William Shakespeare**

After my freshmen year I could truly say that college was everything that I heard it would be and even more of what I dreamt it would be. In fact, my grades were an indicator of just how much fun I had my freshmen year. I traveled more than I had ever traveled in my life and most of my travels were outside of the Midwest. I went as far as I could go and made it back in time for my Monday classes. We went to Nashville, Louisville, Knoxville, Atlanta, Birmingham, Memphis and Miami. I took full advantage of the campus life. I went to every basketball game, played in every spades tournament, played in every intramural sporting event available, never said no to a bowling tournament and missed work as many days on the job as I could without losing my work study job. But nothing made my freshmen experience as memorable as the time I spent with De. We did not have her mother to contend with, I could see her everyday and we even had class together. Our love for each other grew on campus in a way I don't think it could have grown in Detroit. For instance, at least the first two quarters, we would go to church together and some co-ed worship services together and in between classes we would walk through the campus and have worship together. One thing we did not have to worry about was De getting pregnant and having to leave college and go home. All the strict school rules helped us to take our relationship slow and focus on getting to know each other. Huntsville wasn't a big city like Detroit so we spent the majority of our time walking, talking, studying, and getting to know each other on a deeper level.

"I don't want to grow up, 'cause if I did, I wouldn't be a Toys R' Us Kid."

That year I got married, and you couldn't tell me anything. I used to joke with my boys and say, "Take out your cameras and get a snapshot of this, because this, my friend, is what a grown ass man looks like." But it did not take long for reality to set in and bust the air out of my bubble. Once the honeymoon stage ended, it was back to real life. I soon discovered, dreaming is one thing, but at some point I had to get up, get out and get something. Somehow, I had been led astray. I thought all I had to do was dream about how I wanted my marriage and life to be like and from time-to-time share the dream with my wife over a candlelit dinner. But I forgot I married a Detroit sister, and from my experience, they were cut from a different cloth. It did not take long before my wife started in on me. "You call yourself a man, what kind of man plays video games all day? When are you going to fill out a job application and get a real job?" she bellowed. She thought as soon as we got married I was going to make a swift transition from a boy to a man. But somehow I came back to school still immature. Instead of looking for a job I was over my boy's house playing Techmo Bowl. If I wasn't playing video games, I was on campus in a planning session for Bell Tower. What I wasn't doing was handling my responsibilities as a new husband. Until one evening or should I say one early morning, I came home about 2 a.m. from the Bell Tower. The Bell generally ended right at curfew, 10:30, but sometimes we would go to one of the dorms to do a follow up session. This particular night we got into a deep discussion with the twins, Paul and Patrick and afterwards we stopped by the Waffle House. When I walked in the house and eventually in the bedroom, De looked at me and started crying. "What's wrong?" I asked as I sat next to her on the bed. I thought she was having some challenges in the nursing program and that she was probably just a little frustrated because school was so demanding. "It's you." she said with an attitude.

"Me, what did I do?" I asked, confused. I am out here trying to do my thing for the ministry."

"That's the problem, the ministry! Did you marry the ministry or me?"

"I married you," I responded quickly.

"Act like it then! You spend all your time on campus or with your boys while I sit here waiting for you to come home. And what about a job? We can't live off that little money you made over the summer selling magazines. You need to go get a real job!"

She was right, I did need to grow up, get a job and get my priorities straight. I was not single anymore. I made a vow before God and in the presence of at least one witness that I was going to take care of her till death do us part; and not just financially, but emotionally as well. The next morning, bright and early, I put in a couple of calls to my people from Huntsville to see if they knew who was hiring. A couple weeks later I had a few options on the table and I decided to go with the Olive Garden. I chose the Olive Garden because the first busboys shift did not start until 11:00 a.m. and ended no later than 4:00 p.m., which meant I could leave as early as 2:30 to 3:00 p.m. if I was not the head busboy. If I worked second shift, I worked from 4:00 to 6:30 or 7:00 p.m., which meant I could still take morning class and I could make it to the Bell Tower.

I knew working was not enough. I needed to put more

time into my marriage and my spiritual life. However, there were some things I knew I could not afford to sacrifice. The Bell Tower was one of them, Tuesday's Chapel and special spiritual events like week of prayers were another. I needed to attend as many spiritual functions as possible, and I needed to stay active in the Bell Tower because I was beginning to see some serious growth in my program development and my public speaking.

If a man does not work he should not eat.

"Nothing worthwhile comes easily. Work, continuous work and hard work, is the only way to accomplish results that last." - **Hamilton Holt**

Have you ever thrown a pebble in a pond? If you have, then you know what happens. All you see at first is a little splash—nothing more nothing less. But if you pay close attention, seconds later that little splash starts to form circles. It starts as small circles at first but all of a sudden the circles start to expand. Soon the small circles become larger and larger. My rock experience and my experience at the Olive Garden were parallel. What started out as a not so glamorous busboy position catapulted me from an average Joe to the success I enjoy today. It still amazes me to think back on how a little hard work, a little going the extra mile, a genuine smile, a kind word, a yes ma'am, a no ma'am, a how may I help you, and a lot of sweat, blood, and tears opened up windows of opportunity and positioned me for success.

It is amazing to me how obsessed this current generation is with the idea of success. You hear the enthusiasm in their voice when they describe their dream car or when they describe the seven-bedroom, four-bath house in a gated community that they eventually want to move into. However, they get quiet when you explain to them the type of work ethic that is required to live that type of lifestyle. I was fortunate in that I learned at a very young age that there were no free lunches in life. There is nothing wrong with dreaming big dreams, just know that all roads that lead to success have to pass through Hardwork Boulevard at some point. So the day Olive Garden handed me my personal apron, a bucket, and my own cleaning supplies, I knew the deal. Work was more about the process than it was about the money. I made the mistake of thinking it was about the money when I worked at T.J. Maxx, Wendy's, and Burger King. This time I would not make the same mistake. I would prove to myself and to God that I did not need to repeat the test because I had learned the lesson. The way I approached my work was the difference between me being a busboy for the rest of my life or me telling the world how being a busboy was a part of this amazing journey that began years ago. Through trial and error, I had a broader understanding of what work could do for me beyond the money and in return what I could do for the Olive Garden.

When I left the Olive Garden four years after the day I was hired, I can truly say I entered as a boy but I came out a man.

Unusual favor is bestowed on those that work

One of the first things I did to launch my speaking career was embrace the concept of meditation into my life. I decided to dedicate the first hour of the day to speak to and listen to God. I added listening to my meditation time because I hate those one sided relationships. You know the ones where your friend does all the talking and you can't get a word in. One day during my meditation time, God gave me a revelation about work through the following scriptures:

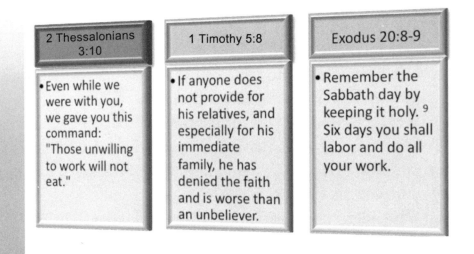

2 Thessalonians 3:10	1 Timothy 5:8	Exodus 20:8-9
• Even while we were with you, we gave you this command: "Those unwilling to work will not eat."	• If anyone does not provide for his relatives, and especially for his immediate family, he has denied the faith and is worse than an unbeliever.	• Remember the Sabbath day by keeping it holy. [9] Six days you shall labor and do all your work.

First and foremost, He revealed that work was a significant aspect of His personal value system. Before He asked me to go to work, He went to work. According to Genesis, even before any signs or miracles were wrought, He worked. I am no genius, but I just believe He could have done in one hour what it took him six days to do. So He modeled what He wanted me to do - work. He specified the time frame so I would not think it was acceptable to work three days and play four days. Then He helped me make the connection between my faith and work. I began to understand that work is an outward manifestation of an inward change. And finally, He said if I am able to work, but unwilling, I should not even eat. Bottom line, a lazy person is not placing himself or herself in a position of greatness. That revelation sealed the deal for me. I knew from that day forward my pay scale was not in man's hand. If God was pleased with my work performance then no one devil in hell could prevent me from getting what He had planned for me.

You have to place yourself in Miracle Territory

When I am trying to convince young people of just how invaluable working is, I often compare it to flying first class. If you have never flown first class before you might be under the impression that it's all hype. You might be saying to yourself, there is really not a big difference between coach, business class, and first class except the price tag. There is a huge difference! I have flown coach on an international flight and I have flown first class. I preferred the first class experience. Besides the obvious, more leg room, wider seats, hot meals, convenient access to the restroom, electrical access, real glass, a hot washcloth, you get the point already; the potential networking opportunities are astronomical!

I discovered the same is true when you are passionate about your work or about the process. It's like flying first class; you place yourself in Miracle Territory. It's not about liking or disliking the company you are employed by. It's not about the relationship between you and your supervisor or colleagues for that matter. It's about taking advantage of the opportunity that has been given. It's about working at your optimal level. And if you are not willing to give one-hundred and twenty percent, then don't get upset when those around you get promotions, raises, and other benefits. You have to realize you can't expect a full harvest when you are not willing to put your best effort forward. Because I understood that concept, I walked in the Olive Garden like I owned shares in the company. I was not a cook and I was too young to wait tables. The law in Alabama stated that you had to be 21 to sell liquor. That did not stop me from learning the entire menu and what each dish contained. I studied everything. I could tell you what was in the salad, both the soups; my favorite was the classic minestrone soup. I could even break down the meat and vegetable dishes.

There was a huge vegetarian population in Huntsville, and I wanted to make sure their experience was unforgettable. I worked hard, and because of that doors began opening up for me. For instance, regular customers used to request that I serve their table even though I wasn't a waiter. I read Dale Carnegie's book, How to Win Friends and Influence People, so I learned that it was important to remember the customers' names and remember their orders. Every time they visited the restaurant and I called them by name and remembered what they generally ordered they felt like they were getting special treatment. Some waiters would request I bus the tables in their area because I did more than what was required. I would take the customers' drink orders and sometimes even their entrees if the waiters were busy. That isn't to say that I never made any mistakes. One night we were short staffed and my boss asked me to take drink orders at a few tables. This one particular table was special to me because there were some local pastors who I recognized and it was an honor to be able to serve them. They all ordered virgin strawberry daiquiris, only I forgot to tell the bartender to make them virgin. Well, after a few minutes I went back to the table to check on them and they all commented on how great the drink was and that they would take another virgin daiquiri. I walked back up to the bartender and said, "four more virgin daiquiris please." "Virgin?" the bartender asked. "You didn't say virgin last time." It turned out that I gave all the pastors a nice big shot of rum! I felt terrible although they seemed to be feeling excellent. I never said anything, and neither did they. I learned a lot during my time at Olive Garden and just as important, I made a ton of great relationships that would benefit me in the future.

CHAPTER
12

What an Experience

"Today you are You, that is truer than true. There is no one alive who is Youer than You." - **Dr. Seuss**

Dorothy was on to something - *"There is no place like home."*

As much as I loved my first year experience at Oakwood, I always felt like a fish out of water. The fact that I was not familiar with a lot of the cultural habits that existed bothered me. During chapel service they sang songs like *"Bye and Bye," "Glory Glory," "The Blood that Jesus Shed," "Precious Memories How They Linger"* and so forth. For the first few months I lip-singed and pretended I knew the songs. Then there were those spiritual sayings they would repeat throughout chapel. It was like they had their own language. The biggest challenge was the cliques. It seemed like ninety percent of the students went to high school together or they had relatives attending the school. There were only a handful of freshmen from Detroit, and I only knew one or two of them on a first name basis because they went to school with De.

It reminded me of my basketball experience. I never truly embraced the game because I did not excel at it. I excelled in football. As a result, I loved the game of football. When it came to a football game, people went out of their way to make sure I played on their team, but when it was time for basketball they would go to the park and not even tell me they were going. College, for me, was a lot like my basketball experience. In order to get the full benefit of college, my academic game had to be tight or I had to at least be able to sing or play an instrument. Unfortunately, I did not posses any of those skills. I believe that is why I gravitated toward the work environment. I not only survived in that environment, I thrived. I had the work ethic that would allow me to become one of the best.

But after working in the real world for a few months, I knew busing tables was not for me. Bottom line, some birds are not meant to be caged. However, for the time being De and I needed the money so I was in no position to quit. From that day forward I purposed in my heart that I would do what I loved doing and not what I was forced to do to make a living.

CHAPTER

13

Enter to Learn, Depart to Serve
- Oakwood College Mantra

We make a living by what we get, we make a life by what we give -**Sir Winston Churchill**

My community service efforts had grown dramatically, from visiting elementary and middle school students, and the elderly, to the developing and implementing a G.E.D. program. I started the G.E.D. program because I felt I had to do more. The G.E.D. was my ticket out of Detroit and my passport to the world, literally, and I felt as if I had a debt to pay to those who helped me. The program specifically targeted mothers who were unable to finish high school due to unplanned pregnancy, and youth offenders, i.e., drug dealers, and gang members.

"I've learned that people will forget what you said, people will forget what you did, but people will never forget how you made them feel." - **Maya Angelou**

When I started the G.E.D. class I did not have a dime to my name or any financial backing but it all worked out because there were only a few mandatory items I needed to get started. I had to have a G.E.D. book, some pencils and pens, some writing paper, scrap paper and a classroom with a few desks. The book, paper, pencils and pens would be the easy part, finding office space would be somewhat challenging. During my devotional time, I prayed to the Lord and asked for wisdom regarding the class space. A few days later my answer came to me as I was driving down University Ave. All of a sudden it dawned on me that there was a neighborhood community center in the complex. I knew there had to be at least a few classrooms that were not being used. When I made it home I called Black to see if he would roll out with me to the center just in case there were a few classrooms available and to find out what the requirements were to lease the space. As fate would have it there was plenty of available space and based on the type of program I was providing the neighborhood, the director was more than happy to accommodate me. Now that the facility was secure, it was time to check off the other items one by one. I bought my first G.E.D.

textbook from Books a Million. I then asked one of my professors for writing paper and the center provided scrap paper and to my surprise they took care of all my printing needs. I had some extra pencils and pens lying around at the house, so I brought those from home. Classes were everyday from 12-4. I wanted to run the classes earlier but I knew it might affect attendance so I encouraged those that needed extra help to meet me earlier or stay after class. I had a gut feeling that this was not going to be your typical group. It was my guess that some of the students would have some mental and emotional challenges they would need to overcome before they ever dealt with their academics struggles. With that in mind, I divided my lesson plan in three segments. Before we did anything we discussed their goals for themselves and my personal goals for the class. The next 10 -15 minutes I read a powerful motivation speech and ended it with an electrical charge that summarized the points of the devotion. I figured I had a better chance of gaining their interest and getting them engaged in the learning experience if I made them feel good about themselves and made them believe that somehow their dreams could come true through hard work. Instead of designing my program with a traditional approach, I added some creative methods. Mainly, I used a team approach. Based on the strength of the students, I assigned each of them a day to teach and I divided my lesson plan with them according to their assigned day. The idea was to keep them as active as possible for the entire class period. I knew it was difficult for a number of them to concentrate on the lesson at hand. For some it was family challenges that kept them from giving me their undivided attention, for others it was the fear that their infants were not in the safest daycare facility. Mothers would repeatedly dismiss themselves from the classroom to call the daycare facility to make sure their child was safe. Had it not been a requirement to pursue their G.E.D. in order to remain on government assistance, there is a chance that many of the mothers would not have enrolled in the program. Then there were my most challenging students. They were either gang bangers or drug dealers who would have also preferred to be elsewhere but were required by the courts to get in a G.E.D. program or return to prison. Regardless of the challenge that prevented them from taking school serious, I felt compelled to find out what learning environment and teaching style most complemented their learning style.

"Before you speak, it is necessary for you to listen, for God speaks in the silence of the heart." - **Mother Teresa**

I learned early in my teaching career that you have to possess a unique set of skills if your plans were to teach students from low-income schools. However, I had no idea I was going to be a teacher, counselor, advisor, mentor, bus driver, motivator and to some, a father figure. Often times I had to veer from my lesson plan to address the real life issues my students faced. The effort I put forth daily to see to it that my students received a first-class learning experience was exhausting. By the time I straightened up all the chairs, picked up the last piece of paper off the floor, wiped the red ink off the eraser board, and counseled two or three of my students, I was ready to drop. I quickly discovered that I had to find a way to replenish myself. There was no way I could put forth that type of energy day in and day out without refueling. So like a star athlete, I added a pre-game warm up routine to my repertoire.

It started with my devotion time in the morning. First, I would pray and ask God for wisdom. As far as I was concerned, God created them so He had a much better sense of what they needed. Two, I spent about 30 minutes envisioning what the class should look like. I actually taught the entire class in my thoughts so when the actual class took place, it wouldn't be my first time teaching it. Then I put together a strong playlist. I used my music to help shape my thoughts on the ride over. I believed that the physical environment played just as much a role in the learning process as the lesson and the teacher. I did not have a lot to work with but I plastered images of great African Americans throughout history in an attempt to inspire my students to reach greatness. My final pre-game routine was to look over the lesson to make sure no changes were needed then I would walk over to the classroom door so I could greet each student with a smile, a hug and a specific word of encouragement to help set the tone of the class.

As time went on, I began to tap into my network and

started building a library of great motivational books and videos from people like Les Brown, Tony Robbins and Zig Ziglar. Whenever I finished with the book or tape I put it in the community center's library so my students could have access to them. I was so concerned with staying pumped up and motivated that I put together an *"In Case of a Rainy Day box."* Black taught me the importance of forecasting challenges so you can cut them off at the root. The box wasn't elaborate or expensive to make. It had little simple stuff in it like my favorite underdog movies, songs, books, poems, and goals for the year. Whenever I felt the slightest bit of discouragement and felt like giving up I would get my *"In Case of a Rainy Day"* box and encourage myself. My philosophy was that your spirit affects your disposition. If my spirits were negative, how would that affect others? So I tried to stay enthusiastic about life and I fought to maintain an upbeat disposition. I wasn't getting paid to teach my students. My only reward was their success so I wasn't about to waste their time or mine.

CHAPTER
14

P.U.S.H

(Push Until Something Happens)

"Never underestimate the importance of the beginning. The beginning has the seeds of everything else to come. Started a G.E.D. program in the hood and the rest was history."

We must accept finite disappointment, but we must never lose infinite hope.

Almost an entire year had passed since I dropped everything to pursue my dream and no results. Not one student had registered for the G.E.D. test. An entire year of preparation and I was unable to convince one student that they needed to take the test. I was starting to believe

I had made a big mistake. Maybe the doubters were right. Maybe I jumped the gun; I should have stayed in school; I kept thinking, maybe I should just throw in the towel and give up the hoop dream. Go get a "real job."

"With every deed you are sowing a seed, though the harvest you may not see." - Ella Wheeler Wilcox

I wasn't sure which was worse, coming to grips with the fact that the program was a complete failure or dealing with the fact that I was succumbing to self-defeating thoughts… again. I took pride in the fact that I was this jubilant, upbeat person, that I was somehow able to rise above negative circumstances and defy all odds. But this one was hard to bounce back from, it knocked the wind out of me. I was no longer living for myself; I was married, so my decision had a direct impact on De. In fact, 6 months after I left my job to pursue my dreams and all savings evaporated, she decided to get a job to help make ends meet. I felt so bad because she was getting up at 5:30 a.m. to make her 6:30 a.m. clinical, stayed in class until about 3:30 and went to work until about 9:30 – 10:00 p.m. I decided the best thing to do for the sake of my marriage was to man up and call the G.E.D. program quits. Next week would be my last week. As that week was coming to an end I pulled all the students together and I made my announcement. "Guys, this has been one of the most enriching experiences of my life, in almost a year our relationship has grown, you each have grown academically and personally. I believe that for each of you the best is yet to come. With that being said, I hate to inform you that next week is my final week. None of you are the reason for my decision. In short, I am leaving for financial reasons. Over the past year I have poured my personal finances into this program and I can no longer afford to live and invest in the program." As soon as I finished one of the most touching speeches of my career, Zanzabar, one of the top drug dealers in the city blurted out, "Did I just hear you say you were quitting? Tell me you're kidding, right? Is this a joke?" he asked. I know "Mr. Don't ever give into defeat" ain't standing here telling us he's 'bout to give up on his dreams over money. I thought you were different Mr. Thomas but you just like the rest of them fake teachers. You don't give a damn about us." I am not sure if I was more stunned or embarrassed. What do you say after one of your students hangs you out to dry like that in front of the entire class? My ego had been slightly damaged, but Zanzabar was right. If there was one thing I tried to instill in them, it was that defeat was not an option, come hell or high water, never be denied and never quit short of the prize. Here I was being a hypocrite. I could not come back from that blow, so I just said, "Have a great weekend and I will see you guys Monday!" I spent that entire weekend to myself. I called on the Lord every waking hour. Father, I'm in a major jam again and I don't know what to do. You said you would never leave me nor forsake me. That I have not because I ask not. Well, I am asking Father. I can't afford to give up on my students but I can't afford to keep doing it for free. Please Lord, show up and show out! Give me some sort of sign that I am doing the right thing. Less than a week later, on one of my last days, two older gentlemen walked through the doors of the community center and into the room where I held my G.E.D. classes. They just stood there and observed me in action. After I dismissed the class the two gentlemen approached me and informed that they represent the Department of Education for the State of Alabama. They said that for the past few months they had been hearing good things about the program and that they wanted to see it for themselves. They were so impressed with what they saw they offered their support. Needless to say, I accepted their help and continued teaching my class. From that day forward they purchased all the computers, software, textbooks, pencils, and took care of all my printing needs. That one act rekindled my belief in my dreams and if that wasn't enough of a sign from God, a few weeks later, God showed up again. One evening De and I were scraping our pennies together for groceries and I felt impressed to pray over the mailbox. So we stopped, got on our knees, looked out the window and thanked God for whatever he was getting ready to do. Even though we were down to our last few pennies I truly felt as if God was about to do something special for us. After we prayed over the mailbox, the mail lady came 2 hours later. I will never forget going to the mailbox somewhat afraid. I kept thinking to myself, what if it wasn't God? How would this affect De's faith in me? As I got closer to the mailbox the spirit of anxiety overwhelmed me. Filled with more faith than fear, I opened the mailbox and grabbed the handful of mail. The first envelope was junk, the second was junk, the third was a bill but there was one more piece of mail that I didn't recognize, so I ripped the edges off the side and when I opened it, it was a check for $285.00. I literally dropped the check and fell to the ground. "Thank you Father, thank you... not only for the check, but for hearing and answering our prayers." To think I had almost given up. If it had not been for Zanzabar's words, I would have removed myself from Miracle Territory and all the blessings that were about to follow.

"Keep on sowing your seed, for you never know which will grow -- perhaps it all will." - **Albert Einstein**

I didn't know much about farming at the time I departed to serve my community. But I must admit, the time gap between sowing a seed and reaping a harvest seemed awfully slow. However, I learned through the process not to make time the focus. The secret to success is in the nature of the seed, not how long it takes to see results. For what you sow you will eventually reap, some seeds just take longer to harvest.

Shortly after receiving the check and gaining financial support for the program, the Huntsville Times newspaper started reporting on my program on a regular basis. Soon after, the local television networks started doing stories on my G.E.D. program, mainly Channel 48 news. I was on every morning show and whenever there was an incident involving at-risk youth I served as the expert consultant. Channel 48 and David Person even did an hour special on my work in the community. The local support started pouring in left and right. Individual donors started dropping off writing and typing paper, pens and pencils and all sorts of books. The biggest support came by way of a group of professional black men who recently formed a nonprofit organization by the name of 20 Distinguished Men of Huntsville. Their founder Lamar Higgins, who at the time was the personal assistant to the mayor, took a deep interest in the work I was doing and offered the organization's support. Two months into my relationship with the organization, they offered me a private office space downtown and helped me to secure multiple grants. With their help, the news of my contributions to the at-risk population in the city grew rapidly. As a result, I was able to establish credibility amongst some of the city's leading businessmen and women. Among them was, Hall of Famer, John Stallworth, the former wide receiver for the Pittsburgh Steelers and a native of Alabama. He graciously absorbed all the cost associated with the G.E.D testing for my students. Another NFL player, Ralph Malone of the Cleveland Browns and also a native of Alabama lent his support. He believed in exposing students to opportunities outside of their neighborhood. He donated funds for field trips to places such as the Space and Rocket Center and other engineer based sites. He also secured tables for the students at elaborate galas and awards shows in order to expose them to a more affluent way of life. As a result of all the support, my students began to thrive. Not only were they now taking the test, many of them were passing with flying colors and moving on to find great jobs!

Trying to Make a Real Difference
COLLEGE STUDENTS PUSH EDUCATION
by JILL RHODES (Huntsville Times Staff Writer)

A younger Eric Thomas was always too busy running with friends, looking for trouble on the streets of downtown Detroit, to finish out his senior year in high school.

Older and more educated now, Thomas was marking up a chalk board recently in the Calvary Hill Community Center, adding and subtracting fractions for an audience of young black men from the Norwood Housing Project nearby.

"When I was 16, school just didn't fit in to my schedule," said Thomas, 22, a senior at Oakwood College. "I was out all the time, running with the boys, getting into trouble, so I dropped out. But one day I talked to the pastor at my church and he said, 'get your General Equivalency Diploma. Go to Oakwood College'."

Malcolm Gopher gets help with a math problem from Eric Thomas, left, and a helper, Lester Smith in class at Calvary Hill Community Center.

STUDENTS CONCERNED

Eventually, Thomas did earn his G.E.D. He was also accepted at Oakwood. But Thomas and a group of friends from Oakwood and Alabama A&M University are going further. Calling themselves the Concerned Black Students, Thomas and his friends invaded the Norwood neighborhood recently to recruit other young black kids — most of them drop-outs from Butler High School — for a GED preparation program the CBS students began on their own.

"I felt like if someone like my pastor could encourage me to get my GED, I could relate that to others who are in the same situation I was in," Thomas said. "Most of the community leaders we've talked to here say this age group, from 16 to 25, is untouchable, that they are unapproachable.

"But that's not true," he added. "And that's what we came here to prove."

Thomas said the group targeted the Norwood neighborhood for the program because other public housing areas in the city seem to already enjoy some form of social improvement support.

In Norwood and the adjacent Love subdivision, however, the CBS group said the prevailing attitude among kids there is apathy — mostly driven by ignorance and a lack of any type of governmental support.

STREET RECRUITING

"We just came in here and approached many of these young men on the street corners," said Irvin Daphins, 20, and an Oakwood student working with CBS. "Eventually, we got them hooked basically by just getting them to know that, at this point, the only way they are going to see a real difference in their lives is to get an education."

The group's goal is to get each of the 12 students now enrolled in the GED preparation class accepted at an area college in the upcoming spring quarter, said Daphnis, who, like Thomas, helps teach the preparation classes three times a week.

And getting the young people interested in the idea, Daphnis added, has so far been a snap, especially since most of the neighborhood kids have been in trouble with the police, come from single-parent homes and have virtually nothing to do all day but roam the neighborhood.

ANOTHER CHANCE

"I just came into the class to stay off the streets," said one of the CBS students, 23-year-old Donald Ford. "I was up here at the community center one day roaming through the halls, browsing around, moping around, doing nothing and (Daphnis) came up to me and said, 'Get your GED'."

Ford finished high school, he said, but did not go to college. Today, Ford has forgotten most of what he learned to make it through college, and has been unable to get a job.

"This is a good thing," Ford said, re-lighting a half-smoked cigarette as he studied his fractions. "I'm looking for a job and it seems no one will hire me. This will help. Plus, I don't have anything else to do with my time."

Like Ford, 17-year-old Fabian Cawthorne is preparing with the CBS group to take the GED test in December. "I want to be an attorney," said Cawthorne, who dropped out of Butler High School in the 10th grade.

"I was a year or two behind in school and everything just got so frustrating, I quit," he said. "If I didn't come to this class, I probably never would have thought about getting a GED."

Although Cawthorne now has 12 classmates, members of the CBS say anyone from any area in the city who wants to improve themselves is welcome.

But the college students said they desperately need more books, more paper, pencils and a copying machine to keep them going.

"These young men are very smart," said Erica Tate, an English major at Alabama A&M. "These students aren't ignorant like a lot of people say they are. They just need someone to motivate and push them."

STARTING AGAIN

One 21-year-old enrolled in the class said he hopes to be a part of the CBS effort soon.

"I'm going to college, to A&M, to be a criminal lawyer, then to law school and this class is the beginning to get there," said Bobby Sledge, who dropped out in the 10th grade.

"It's a wonderful feeling to see black youth my age who care about older black kids come out and do this," Sledge said.

"These guys have never had any encouragement to break the cycle they are in," added Thomas. "If my pastor hadn't told me to get my GED when I was 16, I'd still be in the same situation these young men are in. I feel this class will be their last chance."

In the summer of 1993, I felt so empowered and had so much confidence in my abilities I decided to branch out. Atlanta Georgia was the closest major city so I asked Rio, a good friend of mine from Los Angles, to put a business plan together and help me raise funds for a youth centered event on the west end of Atlanta. I was shocked when we were able to get the attention and support from some of the most prominent black leaders. After having an initial meeting with members of the West End Church, the next thing I knew we were meeting with Joseph Lawry of the SCLC and Pastor Eric Young of the West End Seventh-day Adventist Church. When the meeting ended I could not believe they gave us the seed money to conduct a 4-week youth revival. 1992 was a breakout year for me. Outside of a few meetings with Joseph Lawry and his staff and some weekly meeting with Pastor Young, I was given the freedom to hire my own staff and devise my own personal plan. At the end of the four weeks, I had evolved from a boy to a man professionally. We were a bunch of college students designing activities for the youth, conducting nightly revival services for the community, and managing budgets. I walked away that summer knowing without a shadow of a doubt what my purpose in life was and what population I had been birthed to serve.

CHAPTER
15

White Sands and Blue Water

"Bermuda, Bahama come on
pretty mama." – **The Beach Boys**

Things just kept getting better. That one seed I planted just kept giving and giving. About 2 months after the Atlanta experience, I was sitting at my word processor doing some homework when I heard a knock at my apartment door. To my surprise, it was a family I met at the revival in Atlanta, the James' from Bermuda. They explained that they were visiting their son, my boy Shannon James. We initially made small talk about how much they enjoyed the work I did in Atlanta. They then began asking me about my plans for winter break. They wanted to know if I planned to go home and if so, for how long. I told them I wasn't really sure and that De and I were still trying to figure out our plans. Out of nowhere they pulled out two plane tickets and asked if De and I would be willing to spend a portion of our winter break in Bermuda. They were interested in me doing the same thing for their youth group in Bermuda that I did in Atlanta. They also wanted me to do a small speaking tour for the public and private school system. I sat there thinking to myself, "...*this can't be real.*" Just six months prior to their visit, I specifically dreamt of going to Bermuda. My boy Shawn Crockwell was from Bermuda. When he heard my car broke down and that De and I needed a ride to school, he made it his business to make sure we got to school on time Monday thru Friday. On the way to school he would talk about what life was like growing up in Bermuda. Shawn talked about his love for futbol as a kid, the beautiful weather, the beaches and the food. He didn't realize that while he was sharing what it was like in his world, I was envisioning everything he was saying. One day after a ride with Shawn I thought to myself, "We are going to go to Bermuda to experience what he keeps talking about." Who would have known that a small thought would somehow travel across the Atlantic to the James family in Bermuda and eventually place them in my living room with not one, but two tickets to Bermuda. The next day De and I rushed to Kinko's like two kids in a candy store to get our passports. I learned a valuable lesson about dreaming that year: dreaming alone may not guarantee that all your wishes come true, but it's a hell of a start. The best part is that it doesn't cost a dime to do it.

Bermuda

It was the most beautiful sight I had ever seen in my life. "In preparation for landing, please discontinue the use of all electronic devises; close your tray tables and fasten your seatbelts. We will be landing in Bermuda shortly," the flight attendant advised. "We will be circling the island so for our first time visitors please take out your cameras."

Seconds later, the plane turned as it made its initial decent. Suddenly, I saw the bluest water I have ever seen in my life. As the pilot landed the plane I could see pink, blue and yellow homes, it was unreal. I spent a little over two weeks on the island doing a small speaking tour for Bermuda's school system. I spent the first half of the day speaking to middle and high school students. I tried to drill in their minds the importance of having a dream, setting goals and making the most out of their lives. In the afternoons, I visited at-risk students in youth detention facilities. I was somewhat surprised to see that the kids on the island faced some of the same challenges our inner-city youth experienced. Shocked or not, I didn't hold back one bit. My message was simple and straight to the point: stop the madness. I let them have it and I challenged them to appreciate the opportunities they had. I spent the evenings at a church conducting a youth revival. Talk about an upgrade, my self-esteem and my skill set grew exponentially. My presentations grew stronger after each school visit. I can't explain the feeling I had walking into that auditorium and seeing students staring into my eyes and listening closely to every word I said. When I got back on the plane and headed back to the States, I felt like a millionaire. Less than 4 years ago I was a homeless high school dropout and now I was becoming a successful, international motivational speaker. My thoughts were that, if I can reach the youth and impress the teachers and staff in Bermuda, I should be able to hold my own in the States too.

Don't be content

When I returned to the States, I was hungry for success. I had a taste of the good life, the beach, the food, the money, and I wasn't about to go back to Huntsville and settle for mediocrity. As soon as I landed I got on my grind. I took my G.E.D class to another level. I recruited more volunteers, I purchased more software and I took my recruitment efforts to another level. However, there was one problem. I was putting so much of my time and effort into my speaking career and my community service work that my grades were suffering. By the end of the fall semester of my junior year, I was dismissed from college. From the outside looking in, it may have appeared to be a major setback. In reality, it was a blessing in disguise because neither my head nor heart was in school. Now that I had been dismissed, I had 24 hours a day to invest in my career. Even though I took a lot of flack for getting kicked out, I was determined to prove all of my doubters wrong.

Telephone: Office (809) 292~4753
Fax: (809) 295~5646

The Berkeley Institute
P.O. Box HM 822, Hamilton HM CX, Bermuda

To Whom It May Concern   December 6,1993

Re: Mr. Eric Thomas

I have had the pleasure of meeting Mr. Thomas this week, and hearing him speak to the students on two occasions. I also had an opportunity to hear him on two radio broadcasts over the last week.

On Mr. Thomas' first visit, he spoke to some of our more challenging students, and he was able to capture their attention and challenge them to value their educational opportunities. His message was so profound, and made such an impact on the students that we asked him to return. He willingly consented to come back, and students were begging to hear him again. On his second visit, he spoke with students ranging in age from eleven to seventeen years of age, and he was again successful in motivating and challenging them. Our senior students were so moved that they gave him a standing ovation, and asked if he would consider coming back to be their graduation speaker.They commented that they were not only challenged to be the best they could be, but they were also given a concrete plan of action to ensure success. Another comment from a fourteen year old was,"he has really touched me and made me stop and think about my life and where I am heading".

I have had the opportunity to hear several motivational speakers, and in my experience, Mr. Thomas rates among the best. He was able to communicate with the students on their level, and inspire them to set goals and work hard to achieve those goals. I firmly believe that Mr. Thomas touched many young lives during his visits here, and that they will make some positive changes in their lifestyles as a result.

I commend and thank Mr. Thomas for so freely and willingly giving of himself. Such dedication and selflessness are indeed rare in young men of his age. He not only professes faith in Jesus Christ, but he lives that life as well.

Sincerely,

Mrs. Winifred Simmons
Guidance Counselor,
B.A.,B.S.W.,M.Sc.

155

CHAPTER
16

You Gotta Want It As Bad As You Want To Breathe

"The difference between ordinary and extraordinary is that little extra." Jimmy Johnson

Just when I thought I was doing everything I could do to position myself for greatness, my boy Marcus Flowers came out of nowhere and burst my bubble.

Marcus shared an excerpt of this book that blew my mind and challenged me to reevaluate the meaning of giving 100%. I had just finished speaking at a summer youth camp when I noticed Marcus walking towards me, which was strange because he had already graduated from OC and moved to Atlanta. He was the type of dude that was on his grind so serious that I didn't expect to see him on campus just hanging out. He had recently become a big time promoter in Atlanta. He ran towards me yelling, "E, you gotta read this book. It's off the chain…no, E, you have to read this book like yesterday."

"What's the name of the book?" Before I could get the whole question out of my mouth, he replied, "*Think and Grow Rich: A Black Choice* by Dennis Kimbro." He then started reading this section out of the book about this guru and a young man. The following is my interpretation of the "Guru" story as seen on YouTube's "Eric Thomas-Secrets to Success" video:

The story is about a young man, who wanted to make a lot of money and he decided to go to this guru. He told the guru that, "I want to be on the same level you're on." So the guru said, "If you want to be on the same level I'm on, I'll meet you tomorrow at the beach at four a.m." "The beach?", the young man asked, puzzled. "I said I want to make money; I don't want to learn how to swim."

The guru said, "If you want to make money, I'll meet you tomorrow at four a.m."

The young man got there at four a.m. ready to rock and roll, he's got on a suit, (he should have worn shorts), the old man grabs his hand and says, "How bad do you want to be successful?" The young man says, "Real bad." The guru says, "Walk on out into the water." So the young man walks out into the water (watch this), when he walks out into the water it goes waist deep. The young man is thinking,"… *this guy is crazy… I want to make money and you got me out here swimming, I didn't ask to be a life guard, I want to make money. You got me in...*" The guru interrupted the young man's thoughts and said, "Come out a little further." The young man walked out a little further, the water was right around his shoulder area. The young man is thinking again, "*... this man is crazy,* he's making money, but he's crazy." The guru said, "Come on out a little further." The young man came out a little further, the water was right at his mouth. My guy is like, *"I'm about to go back... this guy is out his mind!"*

So the old man said, "I thought you said you want to be successful?"

The young man said, "I do." The guru commanded, "Walk a little further." The young man came and the guru reached down and dropped his head in, holding him down, the young man starts beating and slapping the water. He had him held down and just before the young man was about to pass out, the guru raised him up. He said, "I got a question for you. When you were under water, what did you want to do?" The young man said, "I wanted to breathe." The guru told the guy, "When you want to succeed as bad as you want to breathe, then you'll be successful."

That one small excerpt changed my outlook on life forever. I thought I was on my A game until I heard that story but I realized in seconds that I had not put out the type of effort the guru was referring to. I talked the talk, I watched the motivation videos, I visited the library on a consistent basis but I just "kind of" wanted it. I did not want it as bad as I wanted to breathe. I had to be honest with myself; there were several areas that I hadn't been giving 120%, and if I wanted to be successful for real, I was going to have to push myself much harder.

There were two areas in particular that I tried to ignore. I hoped that if I worked hard enough on my strengths that it would compensate for, and somehow offset my weaknesses. However, I knew deep down inside that at some point I was going to have to man up and deal with my academic struggles and with the pain associated with my biological father. In fact, after the birth of my first child Jalen, I felt this overwhelming pressure to stop avoiding both. I could no longer ignore the fact that my academic challenges and my unwillingness to forgive my biological father for not being in my life were somehow keeping me from going to that next level in my life. I knew neither would be easy to confront but I wanted to succeed as bad as I wanted to breathe, and if it meant tackling two of the biggest obstacles in my life, then I was willing to do just that.

CHAPTER
17

Careful What You Wish For You Just Might Get It

It's weird how things work but as soon as I put the thought out there, it was like God heard me and was waiting on me. The challenge with my father happened much sooner than I expected it to. I was in Chicago speaking to a group of students at a church called Shiloh on the South side off 71st and Michigan. A few minutes before I was scheduled to speak, I walked out of the main sanctuary towards the bathroom. As I was exiting the sanctuary and entering the lobby, I noticed a male figure that looked just like my biological father. After finding out that the father I had been raised by was not my biological father, I began asking questions. My aunt Cleo insinuated that Gerald, whom I assumed was a family friend, and used to stop by from time to time when I was younger, was my biological father. I vaguely recalled what he looked like, but this guy standing in the lobby looked like him! I began thinking to myself, *"It's not possible."* For one, how would he know I was in Chicago and more specifically, how would he know where I was speaking? The more I stared at him the more I realized he was my biological father, and as much as I didn't want to admit it at the time, he looked a lot like me. I froze and my entire disposition changed. My hands were shaking, my heart was racing and I started feeling sick to my stomach. I was so taken off guard by him showing up that I was contemplating not speaking. I was terrified; I didn't know what to say to him or how to handle the situation. All I wanted to do was run out of the church as fast as I could. I was willing to do anything but face him. So I ran into the bathroom and pretended like I didn't see him. I stayed in there as long as I could before I knew I was next on the program. I must have washed my hands and face at least 20 times trying to regain my composer. I finally got the nerve to come out and speak and I think I was able to pull it off without anyone knowing that I was dealing with a serious crisis. But as soon as I finished speaking everything went blank and the feelings of anxiety overtook me again. I tried everything in my power to get out of that church and pretend as though I never saw him but it didn't work. Just as I was leaving the sanctuary, I couldn't help but look in his direction and as soon as I did we made eye contact. He was standing directly in the middle of the isle way. I tried to stall as long as I could so I spoke to everybody on their way out until finally it was just him and I in the lobby and I had no other choice but to face him. All I remember after that was being so angry I wanted to strangle him. Next thing I knew, I opened my mouth and asked, "Why, why did you abandon me and why didn't you say anything to me all those years? Why didn't you tell me you were my father?" I tried so hard not to let the tears roll that they swelled up in my eyes and protruded beyond my eyelids. "Your mother told me not to say anything to you. I wanted to be in your life so bad but out of respect for your mother's wishes I kept silent." His response pissed me off even more. Just weeks ago I stood in the delivery room blessed to see the birth of my first born son who I loved more than life itself and I couldn't imagine letting my wife or anything else for that matter keep me from my baby. I couldn't understand why he didn't fight for his right to see me. As a father, it just didn't make sense, it just didn't add up. In fear that the tears may start rolling if I blinked, I walked off without saying another word. The conversation, though brief, ripped me apart. As much as I tried to deny it for all those years, I still had a desire to know and have a relationship with my father. It was difficult to admit because over the years I had learned how to suppress my feelings and bury my emotions. However, I knew I had to make a conscious effort to let the healing begin, and I knew there was no way I could move on without being man enough to forgive him. I knew it wouldn't be easy but I made up my mind that day that I was going to open the lines of communication and give him a second chance not only with me, but his grandson as well.

I can't explain it but once I faced my fears of reconnecting with my father, every other struggle I had to confront was a piece of cake. In fact, when the new school year came around I took it upon myself to take the necessary steps to try and get reinstated. I figured if I could overcome that one challenge, I should be able to get back in school and overcome my academic challenges as well.

CHAPTER

18

If I Could Be Like Mike

"Some people want it to happen, some wish it would happen, others make it happen" - **Michael Jordan**

For a while it looked like they had his number. In fact, the Detroit Pistons invented a term for it, "The Jordan Rules," which was a defensive strategy employed by the Detroit Pistons against Michael Jordan in order to limit his effectiveness on offense. Devised by head coach Chuck Daly in 1988, the Pistons' strategy was "to play him tough;" to physically challenge him to try and throw him off balance. The Pistons defeated the Bulls in the 1988 Eastern Conference Semifinals and would go on to beat them the next two seasons in the Eastern Conference Finals. But in 1991, Michael Jordan and the Chicago Bulls reinvented themselves. With the help of their new coach Phil Jackson, they implemented the triangle offense and not only swept the Pistons, but went on to win the Championship. Jordan would dominant the NBA for the next decade. He demonstrated the power of reinventing oneself. After pondering for quite some time about how Mike did it, I finally figured it out. Mike made some minor adjustments to his game. I would eventually model the next phase of my life after Mike in an attempt to become one of the "Greats."

Michael Jordan	Eric Thomas
He was placed in a structured system.	I went back to school and brought more structure to my game.
He went from an individual to a teammate.	I developed a nonprofit organization and hired students to go on the road with me to lighten my speaking burden.
He studied the game on a deeper level and began watching more film.	I became a student of the game by mimicking people who were better at the technical aspects of the game (i.e. promotional material, networking, business cards, etc).

Nobody can make you feel inferior without your consent. It's not who you are that holds you back, it's who you think you're not.

Just as the triangle offense helped Mike dominate the game, I knew deep down that going back to college could help take my speaking to a whole new level. But going back to school would require me to make some professional sacrifices. I was all too familiar with the kind of commitment you had to make and the amount of time you had to devote to your studies in order to do well. My poor study habits were another concern. As long as I could remember, I was never a serious student; I just went to school and never had a real love for learning. My friend Lois, she had that love for academics. When we would go bowling on the weekends she bought her textbooks to the bowling alley. I remember thinking, *"Who does that?" Who brings their books to a bowling alley?"* Between frames, she would grab her highlighter and start taking some serious notes or reviewing flashcards. It never dawned on me that that's what real students do; they study. Students don't do it just for a letter grade or numeric values; they study because it's in them. Lois might have taken breaks during her four-year stay in college, but I never saw it.

Although I had been out of school the last three years and had no proof of any academic progress, my work in the community and the church preceded me, so I wasn't surprised when my advisor reinstated me. She probably figured that I had matured during my extended vacation and that I would make better decisions the second time around. She was right. I managed to finish the school year with a 3.5 G.P.A. I owe at lot of my success that school year to Lois. I knew Lois had the secrets to academic success and all I had to do was sit at her feet and learn her system.

Like MJ, I knew once I learned the new system, there was no stopping me.

The following advice is a result of my conversation with Lois Clay and my personal observation of Michael Jordan:

Get support.

One of the first mistakes I made as a freshman was playing individual ball. I knew I needed help but I was too embarrassed to ask for it. Other students made it seem like getting help was for people who were slow. When I struggled in a class, I just kept it to myself and as a result, I failed. I wasn't going to make that mistake the second time around. In fact, I needed more help this time because I was living off campus and working full-time so resources were not as readily available. Like Mike relied on Phil Jackson, I too relied heavily on my advisor and other faculty to help me devise a game plan to overcome my past defeats. They kept me informed about meetings, study tables, scholarships, and special events that were offered for education majors.

Set up the Triangle Offense.

I saw how effective the peer-to-peer learning experience was from my time with my G.E.D. students. As a result, the first week of class I intentionally identified two other students in each class I could study with. Like MJ, I wasn't interested in putting it all on my shoulders anymore - I needed some help. It just so happened that Frank Dent, T.

Black, and I had classes together. Frank was a beast when it came to test taking. He could break a lesson down in story form and give it an acronym like nobody's business. T. Black was a beast at organizing and scheduling study times. Between the two of them I went from getting a 1.3 G.P.A the semester I was dismissed to a 3.5 G.P.A. both fall and spring semester. Besides the grades, I was more motivated to study when we did it in a group and I felt more compelled to do well because we compared grades at the end of each test. I didn't want to be the one with a C+ when they had the A. Like Mike, I now had great teammates and I wasn't afraid to utilize their skills.

Add weapons to your game.

When MJ entered the league he was known for his highflying dunks that electrified the crowd. While fun and exciting to watch, that style didn't lead to any championships. It wasn't until he added some less exciting but equally lethal weapons to his game that he began to win, and win big. Developing a post game, 3-point shot, and a turn-around jumper, were the things that allowed him to become a champion and the greatest player ever. In the end, the dunks and circus moves just turned out to be icing on the cake. Like MJ, I too wanted greatness so it was time for me to add some new, less exciting, but equally effective weapons. I added the following weapons:

1. Utilizing resources

Taking advantage of the campus resources was one of the ways I made adjustments to my academic game. I sought out a mentor. Kenny Anderson was among many of them. He schooled me on the whole college culture. He said it was like anything else - you have to learn the game so you can successfully compete. That advice helped me get a full scholarship that year. I shared with several of the faculty my work in the community and my short and long term plan with my degree and before I knew it, Dr. Frazier said he would do all in his power to help me get my degree. Lois also shared with me the importance of knowing your professor, which was highly possible at a small school. Some of them attended the same church, shopped at the same stores and were advisors to many of the student driven organizations so there were plenty opportunities to connect with them. There were the traditional office hours in which you could meet with the teacher outside of the regularly scheduled class time. I found office hours extremely helpful, especially in the classes I struggled in.

2. Maintaining a balance

Maintaining a balance was another secret Lois taught me. I always wondered how she maintained such a high G.P.A. and graduated magna cum laude. When I paid closer attention, I picked up on her secret. Whenever there was a function, she would devote the first few minutes to her studies. Instead of waiting for the fashionably late people to show up, she studied in the meantime. And when everything was wrapping up, she did not just sit there, she cracked open her book. It was like she was always waiting for an opportunity to study. Between academics, work, family, and social commitments it was important for me to find a way to balance those competing demands. Creating a schedule was key to my success. I hated writing things down, it was frustrating to try to keep up with a pen and planner but it worked. There is nothing magical about a planner, it works because it helps you organize all your tasks and it keeps you accountable.

3. Establishing a routine time to study for each class

One of the things I learned from teaching the G.E.D. program was the importance of consistency. My students did better when we stuck to a routine and it was important that I incorporate that principal as well. Homework was another point I drove home. I taught my students that class was just the warm up. They would not dare play in a big basketball game or football game without warming up or practicing before the game. The same was true with learning. What I taught in the classroom was the appetizer not the entrée. If they really wanted to pass the G.E.D. test, the real work did not begin until they studied away from class. I told them that for every hour they spend in class, they needed to study two hours outside of class. I incorporated that strategy into my game plan as well. I made sure my routine consisted of studying for each subject at the same time and even the same place. My study routine also included more than just doing the assignment. I reviewed my notes from class, and even studied the syllabus daily to see where I was and how far I had to go. If I had spare time once I went through my entire routine, I would prepare for all my classes as if there was going to be a pop quiz. And as a former procrastinator, I always had to remind myself not to put off what I could do today.

4. Discovering my learning style

By discovering my learning style I was able to study effectively rather than just "winging it." After taking a learning style test, I found out that my learning style was:

Verbal/Linguistic Intelligence
Has the ability to use words and language. These learners have highly developed auditory skills and are generally elegant speakers. They think in words rather than pictures.

Their skills include:
Listening, speaking, writing, story telling, explaining, teaching, using humor, understanding the syntax and meaning of words, remembering information, convincing someone of their point of view, analyzing language usage.

Possible career interests:
Poet, journalist, writer, teacher, lawyer, politician,

translator

Take the time to research the learning style that works best for you. Trust me; it makes a world of difference.

5. Take care of your body

Most students do not realize how connected their diet is to their academic life. I had to learn the hard way that studying on four hours of sleep and an empty stomach or junk-food was a sure fire way to keep you struggling academically. I realized getting 6 to 8 hours of sleep, drinking 8 glasses of water a day and exercising helped me immensely when it came time to study. I had more energy, could study longer hours in one setting, and I retained more information. During test weeks I avoided fast food, ate more fruit and vegetables and stopped drinking soda because it had so much sugar and caffeine.

Summary: Points for Academic Success

- Get support.
- Set up the triangle offense.
- Add weapons to your game.
  - Utilizing resources.
  - Maintaining a balance.
  - Establishing a routine time to study for each class.
  - Discovering your learning style.
  - Taking care of your body.

CHAPTER

19

Don't cry over spilled milk. Wipe it up and pour yourself another glass.

My return to college in the fall of 95' proved to be my best academic year ever. I made the Dean's list for the first time in my college career without the help of any remedial courses and I raised my cumulative G.P.A. Things were going great! Based on my conversation with my advisor, I was projected to graduate with my degree in Education May '97. I could taste it and I wanted it as bad as I wanted to breathe. In the midst of all my success, I kept telling myself, "...it's just too good to be true." I wasn't trying to jinx myself; I just had a hard time believing I was finally over the hump. I felt like the Evans family on the T.V. show *Good Times*. Whenever it looked like they got a big break and were finally on their way out of the ghetto, something bad happened. I must have been a distant relative of the Evan's family because it seemed as though I couldn't catch a break, or when I finally did, something would happen to derail it.

Case in point, when I found out I was being reinstated, I knew I couldn't afford the tuition. So, I prayed and asked God to bless me and he came through in a major way. I am not sure how it all happened. One minute I was meeting with a financial-aid counselor, and the next minute someone sends me to Trevor Frazier's office, the master of Pastorial Studies at Oakwood, and he gave me a full scholarship. At that time, I had a 1.7 G.P.A. Talk about a miracle! Later, I heard through the grapevine that he was leaving the University at the end of the school year to pursue his PhD. That could only mean one thing: no Frazier, no scholarship. I thought to myself, *"...here we go again."* This made me question whether I wasted an entire year sitting in class instead of developing myself as a speaker. What about graduation? What about my career? How am I supposed to take care of my family? I loved the community work I was doing but it didn't generate income and although the speaking engagements were picking up, it wasn't steady income either. It was a blessing that De had started her career but we were so swamped with old bills the money was spent before her checks even came in. It felt like someone knocked the wind out of me. Once again I was at a point in my life where I needed to make a

THE SECRET TO SUCCESS

decision. Was I going to let the bad news get the best of me and destroy the momentum I built or was I going to take the lemons life was throwing at me and make lemonade? I would be lying if I said it didn't hurt because it did. So I acknowledged the hurt, went through the whole gamut of emotions, and then moved on.

A Setback is a Setup for a Comeback

After the disappointment of my scholarship not being continued, I got a major break. Kenny Anderson called me and asked if I could present the work I was doing with high school dropouts at the Southeast Center for Human Relations' National Conference on Race & Ethnicity in American Higher Education (NCORE) in Atlanta. The invitation was huge because NCORE didn't invite me. In fact, they didn't even know my program existed. Kenny was the one they invited and he was willing to give me ten minutes of his time. He invited me because he wanted those in attendance to see that there were young black men doing positive things in the community and that the media should spend just as much time highlighting stories like mine as they do the negative stories. I thought the best way to utilize the opportunity was to let two or three of the G.E.D. students speak directly to how the program impacted their lives. One of the girls was a teenage mom who had received her G.E.D., got a job and was in college. Another was a young man who was previously in and out of jail and in gangs and had now turned his life around. After I spoke, the place went bananas and my career as a public speaker took off. At least three high profile engagements came out of that one invitation and created the momentum that I am still riding to this day. The first invitation was from Dr. Eric Abercrombie who invited me to speak at University of Cincinnati's Black Man Think Tank. The second invitation was from the director of Diversity magazine. He invited me to be a guest on their annual teleconference. The third invitation came from Mrs. Juanita Smith. She invited me to speak at Florida A & M's Black Student Retention Conference. After that, the calls started pouring in. There were two engagements specifically that meant the world to me. The first was an invitation by Dr. Joseph McMillan, founder of the Black Family Conference at the University of Louisville. Dr. Mac invited me back every year and he and the Black Family Conference staff adopted me as one of their own. The second invitation would change my life forever. It was from Rodney Patterson and Murray Edwards of Michigan State University.

I broke into the speaking circuit and was finally able to make a living doing what I loved but I knew I wouldn't be satisfied. This wasn't the entire vision, just part of it.

University of Cincinnati

Dr. Eric Abercrombie founded the Black Man Think Tank. I still get goose bumps just thinking about my first standing ovation before a huge crowd. There were approximately 1,800 professionals in attendance. When I walked on stage, all I could see was the stage light shining in my face. I kept telling myself to relax. Just like we rehearsed, all you have to do is remember how we rehearsed it and it will all be fine. I specifically requested a lapel microphone so I could be free to move around and use my body as a prop. It was the fastest eight minutes of my life. As soon as I finished my last words everyone in the room started clapping and one by one stood to their feet. As I exited the stage, I passed by a mirror, I stopped, looked at myself and thought, "I am proud of you, they gave you a shot and you nailed it." During the intermission, I went out in the lobby for a meet and greet. I passed out a ton of business cards and received about ten other speaking engagement offers. None was more meaningful than the offer to speak at Michigan State University. The thought of leaving Detroit as a homeless, high school dropout and returning home to lecture at one of Michigan's finest institutions was overwhelming.

University of Louisville and Michigan State University

I was able to distinguish very early in my speaking career that different institutions had different intentions for inviting me to their campus. Some institutions invited me to their campus to motivate their students, nothing more nothing less. Then there were institutions like U of L and MSU that had a much broader vision. The late Dr. Joseph McMillan of U of L founded the Black Family Conference, which began in 1978. Rodney Patterson and Murray Edwards founded the Black Male Conference at Michigan

State.   Both conferences drew education personnel, parents, community leaders and researchers from around the country to discuss issues affecting African American families and communities.

I presented every year until both conferences were eventually discontinued because of funding issues. I was disappointed that the conferences had come to an end. However, because of the strong relationship I built at MSU with Rodney and Murray, they offered me the opportunity to finish my 4-year degree at MSU, or to attend graduate school there if I finished my undergraduate elsewhere.

MICHIGAN STATE
U N I V E R S I T Y

April 20, 1995

Mr. Eric Thomas
Director, Concerned Black Students
225 Spragins, Suite H
Huntsville, Al 35805

Dear Eric,

Words cannot express our gratitude for what you contribute to our 7th Annual Black Male Conference. The Michigan State University community, students and professional people from all over the state are still buzzing about your electrifying presentation. I don't think people anticipated just how powerful you would be when we originally asked you to participate.

In the previous six year history of the conference, we have been unable to contract a speaker capable of capturing and sustaining the attention of our diverse audience. Because we attract a blend of young teenagers and seasoned professionals, most speakers either direct their speeches toward the professionals, or the youth. You however, managed to speak to both audiences simultaneously, while never losing either group. That is an unusual skill.

I was also impressed with your desire to engage with people and mingle among the conference attendees during the conference. Its not often that a speaker wishes to be accessible to folks. This truly speaks to your genuine interest in people.

Finally, I was most taken by your depth of spirituality and sensitivity. You are a remarkably compassionate and deeply rooted individual. At such a young age, you provide a model to even older men. Our campus will not be the same as a result of your visit. In fact, our students, community agents and churches are already making plans to bring you back to Lansing.

OFFICE OF
**MINORITY
STUDENT
AFFAIRS**

Michigan State University
538 Student Services
East Lansing, Michigan
48824-1113
TOD/A/VOICE: 517/353-7745
FAX: 517/432-1495

Sincerely,

Murray Edwards
Chairperson
Statewide Conference on the Black Male

ME:svb

Enclosures

181

CHAPTER
20

Miracle Territory

Now faith is the substance of things hoped for, the evidence of things not seen – **Hebrew 11:1**

I was driving through campus one day during my lunch break and I noticed the president of the university, Delbert Baker, standing on the curb by the Physical Plant building. I pulled over and asked him if everything was okay. He said that his car was in the shop and he needed a ride to the mechanic. What were the chances that the President of the university is standing on the corner needing a ride just as I am passing by? I knew God had placed me in Miracle Territory again. He told me his wife had been telling him about the impact I had on their youngest son Jonathan. Jonathan was deep into the Bible but struggled with the content of certain textbooks. I decided to use some of the religious materials he enjoyed to teach him the lessons as opposed to asking him to learn it in the traditional way. Not only was his interest in school rekindled, our relationship grew. As we drove on President Baker asked me why I hadn't finished my degree and I responded that it was because of financial struggles. A few minutes later, he made a phone call and I had a full, all expense paid scholarship to finish the rest of my degree. He hooked me up with a work-study position in the Office of Recruitment. My job was to travel to high schools throughout the country and recruit students to Oakwood. I was truly in Miracle Territory, and this time I had no plans on leaving.

The thing I love about Miracle Territory is that it is always so random. It usually happens when you least expect it. One day I was in church enjoying service when Mrs. Pressely walked up beside me and asked, "Eric, can I talk to you after church? The school is interested in having you speak to the student body sometime next week?" I didn't have any other commitments so I told her I would love to do it. The session went very well and the following week I met with the principal, Mrs. Fryson about taking a position as a substitute teacher. She explained to me that the English teacher had broken her ankle and they needed a replacement until she recovered. I was originally told the teacher would be out for about five to six weeks. Two months had passed and she still hadn't returned. Mrs. Fryson eventually hired a new English teacher and offered me a fulltime position as the speech and drama teacher for the remainder of the year and the following year. I gladly accepted.

Oakwood Academy

I am a firm believer that good things do happen to good people; it's just a matter of timing. Those four years in the projects helping high school dropouts get their G.E.D. paid off in a major way. It gave me over five years of experience in the classroom. Even though I didn't have my college degree at the time I was still hired by Mrs. Fryson because of that experience. She told me when she reviewed resume that she based her decision on several factors. One factor was the impact I had on students. In less than half a year I was able to help a number of failing and borderline students regain the confidence in their academic abilities as well as get them excited about learning. Another was that fact that I was back in school and only a few semesters from completing my degree. After all those years of working primarily for free, I could finally tell De that I had my first real job with benefits!

Those few years at the academy were huge. For one, Mrs. Fryson's decision to hire me elevated my confidence in a major way. Oakwood was a small community so it was no secret that some of the more influential members of the school board disapproved of her decision to hire me. That made me work that much harder for her. She pushed me professionally and personally but she never tried to box me in. Instead, she created a structure that harnessed my creativity and supported my unconventional teaching style. I will always be indebted to her for believing in me and giving me a chance when others were not willing to do so.

The love and support I received from my students also helped shape me as an educator. They trusted me enough to embrace my untraditional instructional style and respected me to the point that they made every attempt possible to reach the standards I set. We cried together, we traveled together, we laughed together, and more importantly we grew and matured together.

It would be impossible to share my entire teaching experience in this book. But there are some specific reasons I was able to experience a high level of success working with my students.

Tip 1: Build a relationship

After struggling early with some of the more challenging students in my class, I sought advice from a mentor who had been working with troubled youth for a number of years. The advice was simple yet game changing: "They don't care how much you know, until they know how much you care." It's not uncommon for these students to be abandoned by one or more parents, and that often leads to a mistrust of adults. I decided to take a personal interest in my student's life. I stayed after school a day or two a week and got to know them. Sometimes we would play a little basketball or I would simply ask questions about their life at home. How are your siblings doing? How did your basketball game go the other day? Simple questions like that allowed the student to see that I cared about them not only academically but personally as well. I saw how demonstrating that type of interest went a long way not only in my relationship with the students but its affect on their academics.

Tip 2: Remember each student is different

While it is important as educators to use our past experiences to deal with future situations, remember that no two students are the same. Early in my career I was guilty of placing certain expectations on a student because I recognized similar behavioral patterns from previous students that I struggled to reach. For example, if I had two students with anger issues that failed to thrive in my class the previous year, the next year I automatically assumed that there was no possible way to reach the student who demonstrated similar personality characteristics. By making that assumption, I often failed to make a legitimate attempt at maximizing the students learning potential, instead choosing to focus on the students who "had a chance to succeed." My thought processes were quickly redirected through a number of "success stories" (including my own), and from that day forward, I treated each and every student as a unique individual.

Tip 3: Find a balance

Like so many new teachers, I made a critical error. That error was trying to be the "Cool Teacher." Being young and naïve I figured I would waltz in the classroom with my hip-hop approach and the students would automatically respond to me because of my swag (although back then it wasn't swag, it was...fresh). While it was true that the students loved being in my class, it wasn't because of my depth of knowledge and intellectual creativity, it was because I was a pushover. By refusing to discipline students in fear that they may not think I was a cool teacher, the students ran circles around me. However, I observed teachers with the exact opposite style, yelling and screaming at the students, writing referrals and sending students to the office, and they too failed to positively impact their students academically. By the second semester, I discovered a balance that is still effective to this day. I set the tone in the class. I was the teacher and they were the students. I made the rules and they followed the rules. I set high expectations and they did their best to reach them. I acknowledged their accomplishments and affirmed them every opportunity I had. There were some casual moments in the classroom but I also made sure there were tough and focused moments.

Tip 4: Create an energetic learning environment

One of the most difficult tasks when dealing with grade school students is figuring out a way to harness the massive amount of energy that accompanies children under the age of 12 years. I often found myself dreaming of a classroom where I was able to execute my lesson plan without interruptions; the kids sat down the entire day, remained on task and didn't have to use the bathroom every 30 seconds. I quickly realized that these thoughts were just a fantasy and soon discovered a way to use their energy to my advantage. By creating an energetic learning environment where students were encouraged to use their energy for problem solving and learning, my student's performance quickly accelerated. Using a balance of collaborative learning and individualized learning methods with icebreakers, quiz bowls and jeopardy games, all while keeping the energy high pace and fun, my students began to gravitate towards learning and quickly went from a "Do we have to?" attitude to a "Can we please?" attitude. I also incorporated a heavy culturally relevant pedagogy to make their learning experience more engaging. In short, a culturally relevant pedagogy uses "the cultural knowledge, prior experiences, frames of reference, and performance styles of ethnically diverse students to make learning more relevant and effective for students. It teaches through and to the strengths of these students. It is culturally validating and affirming." Therefore, create the environment that challenges and allows your students to be creative and critical in their thinking, trust me you'll thank yourself later.

Tip 5: Involve the parents as much as possible

One of the most difficult challenges I faced while working in a low-income school was trying to get the parents involved in their student's academic life. As I stated earlier, many of these students come from a single parent home (usually mom) and the parent often does not have the time to check on his or her child during school hours. One of the ways I was able to combat this issue was by making positive phone calls home. I realized that the only time I ever made a call home was when a student was failing or had poor classroom behavior. It never dawned on me that positive calls could have a positive impact on student improvement. Not once in my first year of teaching did I call home to tell a parent that their child did an excellent job in class and that I wanted them to acknowledge the child the first chance they had. As it turns out, parents are much more likely to have a conversation with you when their child is doing well than when their child is doing poorly. By taking small steps like making positive calls home, I was able to build a rapport with the parents. As a result, when it was time to make the "your child is struggling call" they were much more willing to listen and take action.

Tip 6: Be a Life Long Learner

I had to come to the conclusion that professional development was the missing link and the key to my success as a teacher. Once the school year ended, I read every book I could get my hands on about best practices for good teachers. *The Marva Collins Way* was the first book I researched. Her works highlighted the practical yet innovative strategies teachers can use to bring the best out in all students despite their academic background. When I wasn't reading, I was watching every film out about success in the classroom. I had an unusual ability to use films (like most people used workshops or other professional development sessions) and apply them to my practice. The two films that resonated most were *Lean on Me, Stand and Deliver Jamie Escalante.* Both films demonstrated how educators could serve as real change agents by using aggressive, proactive and innovative strategies for school improvement. In addition to what I learned from outside research, I learned a great deal from my own students. I quickly learned that students have a wealth of knowledge about what works and what doesn't work in the classroom. I eventually pulled a few interested students to the side and involved them in the creative process of designing the lesson plan and other related issues.

Tip 7: Give students a sense of purpose

One of the things that concerned me was the lack of interest a number of my students had in the learning process as a whole. I always believed that there was a direct connection between student performance and student interest. A number of my students who had academic challenges were more than capable of excelling. The problem was that they didn't see the benefits of school. I made it my business to help students make the connection. I brought guest presenters from different professional backgrounds to share their story. Mason West and I also created a theatrical group called *Act'in Up* that traveled with me during my college tours. On the academic side, I started a reading initiative for upperclassmen called the *Billion Dollar Book Club,* which encouraged students and rewarded them for reading. These small initiatives ignited the school's spirit and created a bond between the school's staff and the students. Once students made the connection to how school could have a positive impact on their lives, their whole approach to learning changed for the better.

Summary: Effective means of working with students. Tips 1-7.

- Build a relationship.

- Remember each student is different.

- Find a balance.

- Create an energetic learning environment.

- Involve the parents as much as possible.

- Be a life long learner.

- Give students a sense of purpose.

CHAPTER
21

Homecoming

Do you think about me now and then?
Do you think about me now and then?
'Cause I'm coming home again.

Do you think about me now and then?
Do you think about me now and then?
Oh, 'cause I'm coming home again.
Maybe we can start again. **- Kayne West**

By 1998, I had everything I could ask for. My marriage was going great, my career was on the rise, I had a great position on campus, and I was back in school with my degree on the horizon. I also had my second child, my baby girl, Jayda. Life was great but school was challenging. I remember being so frustrated I would have to put my books down and do what I called the "You can do it" visualization exercise. I pretended that I was at my graduation. It was simple because I had gone to every graduation since I arrived on campus. One reason I went every year had to do with the fact that I felt as though I needed to support my friends. Another had to do with the fact that I needed it to burn. It hurt to see my peer's siblings and younger cousins graduate before me. I enrolled at Oakwood in '89 and here it was '98. Each time I attended the ceremony it cut like a knife, but that's exactly what I needed it to do. I learned that pain produces certain things that complacency can't. So when I was tired of studying, I would put my books down and walk through the living room pretending I had on my cap and gown. Then I heard the announcer say, *"Graduating with a bachelors of science from the College of Business. Mr. Eric Thomas."* I was so motivated after that exercise, I would run back to my study area and put another two hours into my books.

I finally completed my degree 12 years after enrolling in college. As I put on my cap and gown I looked in the mirror and began crying tears of joy. I thought about all the cold nights sleeping in abandoned buildings in Detroit. I thought about the moment I found out who my biological father was. I thought about my wife and kids and how proud I was to be a father and husband. I thought about Bob and all the other people who had poured into me when I was at my lowest point. At that moment a calm came over me. It was a feeling I had never experienced. It was a feeling of ultimate peace. I was no longer being held back by my thoughts of academic inadequacy. I was no longer mad at my mother or my biological father. I was no longer mad at myself for the foolish decisions I had made in the past. At that moment, I realized that God had a true plan for my life all along. I understood that he birthed me to be a champion for the underdog. To be that champion, he needed to put me through the fire so that when I speak to people who are at their lowest point, with seemingly no way out, I can honestly tell them that it is possible to rise up and succeed.

Months later, I began thinking about the opportunity Rodney and Murray at MSU had offered me in regards to graduate school. It was consuming my thoughts. I kept saying to myself, *"...even though you never finished high school and barely managed to finish your bachelor's degree, wouldn't it be crazy to give graduate school a shot?"* But that would mean leaving everything De and I had worked for behind for a graduate assistantship that paid little. That would mean leaving our house, De's job, my influence in the city, and all of our family and friends behind. *"Am I willing to make that kind of sacrifice?"*

Hesitant, because I knew it was going to sound crazy, I talked to De that night about my thoughts of attending graduate school at Michigan State University. She laughed at first because she thought I was joking. Once she realized I was serious, the discussion heated up. De was trying to convince me that we had everything we dreamed of having as teenagers, a house, family, secure jobs, and a community of friends who love and support us. I explained to her as best I could that I was positive that this was what the Lord was calling me to do. To which she replied, "Well why don't you go up there and get settled and the kids and I will come up when you get everything in order?"

"No De!", I was adamant. "There is no way that I can do this without you and the kids. Ya'll are my life and I need you by my side if I am going to make this work." Reluctantly, De agreed to leave everything we had worked for behind in order to pursue a new opportunity in Michigan, the place where it all began.

The next morning I went online and downloaded an application from the College of Education's master's degree in K-12 Educational Administration with an emphasis in leadership. I waited for months, checking my mail every day. Finally, I received a large green and white package with a Michigan State University insignia. My heart began to race just as it did with the G.E.D. letter and the Oakwood College letter. I opened it. It read:

Dear Mr. Thomas,

Your application for admission to the Master's degree program in K-12 Educational Administration has been reviewed. I am pleased to inform you that you have been recommended for admission...

Epilogue

I finished my Master's degree two years later, and as I write this, I am a semester away from completing my PhD coursework at Michigan State University. Imagine that, "Dr. Eric Thomas." Has a ring to it doesn't it? We all face challenges in this world, and life is certainly not always easy. But as the expression goes, "It's not about the hand you're dealt, but how you play your cards." Looking back, there is no way I could've imagined my life being so fulfilling. I am still happily married to De, my kids are growing up fast, and I love what I do for a living.

If I could have you take just one thing from this book, it would be that there is no magical formula for success. It's about having a dream and working towards it no matter what negative circumstances occur along the way. In basketball there is a saying that says, "The only way to get out of a shooting slump is to keep shooting." The same can be said for our lives. The only way to get out of mediocrity is to keep shooting for excellence.

Always remember that success is not a destination, it's a journey. To this day I still hear more "No's" than "Yes's." The difference between me then and now, is the fact that the "No's" don't frustrate me anymore. Now, the "No's" actually serve as motivation for the next endeavor.

We all have the ability to produce greatness in our lives. Not one single person on this earth is exactly like you. This means, not one person on this earth can do, exactly what it is that you were born to do. What were you born to do? That is a question only you can answer.

E.T.

A Message From The Author

For almost two decades Eric Thomas' ministry has been a catalyst for developing personal pride and responsibility through positive change in the lives of millions. Through administration, aggressive education, and training programs Eric Thomas empowers people with skills needed to realize and sustain their piece of the "American Dream." Without positive and consistent intervention, the cyclical nightmare of poverty, hopelessness, and despair will be the only realized "American Dream" for people and their children.

It has been found through sociological research that there is a profound link between an individual's destructive behavior and the lack of resources available to them. Without exposure to opportunities, resources to educate, and a strategic plan to use and implement them, the disparity that exists in our society will continue to threaten the growth of our nation.

This concept can be used in various aspects of individual lives. It takes a leadership mentality to change a life perspective and you must be the change you want to see.

[Excerpt from Eric Thomas' new release, *Greatness Is Upon You*]

<u>WEEK 1</u>

"Character is like a tree and reputation like a shadow. The shadow is what we think of it; the tree is the real thing."

Abraham Lincoln

WILL THE REAL ___ PLEASE STAND UP?

It seemed like an ordinary day.

It seemed like an ordinary day. I was sitting at my desk finishing up some paperwork for one of my clients to help him receive special funding for an upcoming project. Just as I was heading

over to the fax machine, I heard a knock at the door. "It's open," I said. It was my boss, Mrs. Paneros.

"Good morning, Eric," she said while standing in the doorway. "How are you today?"

Something about her smile let me know that, while she asked the question, she wasn't really looking for the answer. Still, I responded, "Things couldn't be better. Just getting ready to send this fax off, and then I'm headed out the door to meet with some of my clients before the program tonight."

"Oh ok, sounds great." she said. That's weird, I thought to myself. I knew she wasn't too fond of me spending so much time working on this particular program because she didn't see the value in it, and, normally, the very mention of it would send her into a series of socially acceptable convulsions. She never said it, but I knew she figured that if I was spending so much time working on a non- mandated program, that I couldn't possibly complete my mandated work at a high level.

"Can I see you in my office before you head out?" she asked.

"Sure, I'll be right up after I send this fax. Is everything ok? Do you need to talk about it now?" I pressed.

"Oh, no. Everything's fine, you can just finish up here, and I'll talk to you when you come upstairs," she said.

It seemed like an ordinary day. As soon as I finished sending the fax, I jumped on the elevator and headed to her office. When I got to the door, I noticed that it was partly opened. All I could see was her desk and the huge window overlooking an old creek that had dried up during the hot Alabama summer. Even though I was invited and the door was ajar, I didn't want to be rude and barge in, so I knocked. "Hey, Eric," she said as though she wasn't just in my office a few minutes ago, "come in and have a seat."

I walked into her office, completely oblivious to the reason she wanted me there to begin with. We had our differences before, but we hadn't had any confrontations in literally months. As far as I was concerned, the past was in the past and all was well. As I approached my seat, I noticed that she wasn't alone. On the other side of the door was her boss, Mr. Swanson.

"Eric, I believe you know Mr. Swanson," she said. I had met him a few times before at formal fund-raising dinners but never had any real dialogue with him. "Absolutely," I said, while reaching out my hand.

"He will be monitoring our conversation today," she said, positioning her glasses on her nose.

At that moment I felt the atmosphere shift.

"Mr. Thomas, we want to let you know that you are being written up for insubordination and purposely ignoring company policy. You're failing to live up to the expectations we had for you when you were hired".

I could hardly believe what I was hearing. Over the past year, I had worked my butt off to make sure the needs of my clients were met. I was arriving to work early and leaving late, taking on special projects and creating new ones, all the things that I was told were required as a part of my job.

"What?" I asked stunned, unable to wrap my mind around an articulate response.

"We've explained to you several times that there is a certain way in which we conduct business around here, and you continuously fail to meet the criteria." She then went on about how I purposely mismanaged paper-work in an attempt to make the office look incompetent. Then came accusations about how I had rallied some of the other co- workers in the office to rebel against her and her policies in an attempt to create an unstable work environment.

This was no longer an ordinary day. I couldn't believe what I was hearing! I could feel beads of sweat popping up on my neck as I grew increasingly angry.

"None of this is true, I ..."

"We have it all here in your files," she interrupted, "and we are going to be forced to go public with this and let you go. But if you confess to insubordination and submit your resignation now, on your own, you can walk away. No one outside of this room will ever know that we had this conversation. I would think this through carefully, Eric. The negative press and public humiliation that you could avoid alone makes my offer worth it. Take a few days to think it over."

This was the day that I learned the difference between character and reputation. Even though the next few days were full of rumors about the meeting and all the many implications, I didn't go out of my way to defend myself. Neither did I attempt to spit venom at my superiors for what I considered to be a misguided personal attack. Instead, I showed up to work every day with the same smile on my face, ready for the next challenge, unfazed about what could possibly happen or not happen if my reputation was slandered by lies and deception.

I would be lying if I didn't say that not worrying about my reputation was a harder road to take. When I was younger, I am confident that my anger and need to be seen a certain way would have gotten the best of me. But that day, I realized that there was nothing that I could say or do that would have more of a lasting impact than focusing on my character. I knew who I was, I knew my principles, and I understood that if I remained committed to those things, then nothing external to that made a difference; and so I decided that, for the rest of my life, I was done with feeding into other people's perceptions of me. From that day forward, whenever I was faced with a personal attack, I would let my character do all the talking for me. Let's just say that I walked out of the office, and my new strategy combined with my work ethic ended up working out. Within 11 months, I was promoted not once... but twice within the same company!

What's more important to you, reputation or character?

DAY ONE: LEARN IT

Look, I'm not trying to be deep, but in order for a shadow to exist, it needs something to give it life (i.e., a light source) (Fig 1). The same is true for reputations. Reputations need a light source - someone or something to give it life. This source can be gossip, low self-esteem, unresolved anger, deceptions, desires, disappointments, misconceptions, or misunderstandings.

> Reputations need a light source - someone or something to give it life.

For example, someone with low self-esteem can have a reputation of being a jerk; a series of rumors can misguide people into believing someone is a thief when they really aren't. Because of this, you can have multiple reputations at any given time. When I was young, many people believed that I was skeptical, aloof, untrusting, and (because of my lack of interest in school at the time) unmotivated. For me, my father not being in my life cast a shadow of insecurity and inadequacy that played out in my academic career and many of my relationships.

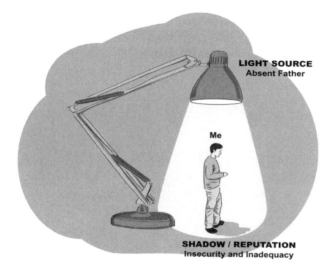

Fig. 1. Shadow Effect

Before I reconciled my relationship with my father, I had some major trust issues and submitting to authority was difficult for me. I was acting out because I was unhappy and this affected my reputation. But as my desires changed, specifically, after I met my wife, got my GED, and started college, I needed people to see me differently; I wanted people to think that I was strong academically; I wanted people to say that I was easy to get along with; and it became important that people thought of me as a "good" guy. My reputation changed, perhaps for the better, but nothing about Eric Thomas had changed. As harmless as this seems, I eventually realized...

DAY TWO: ACCEPT IT

Have you accepted the fact that your success is not about what people say about you but more about who you are?

CHARACTERISTICS OF REPUTATION AND CHARACTER

REPUTATION	CHARACTER
Temporary	Eternal
Rust	Rust Proof
Weak Foundation	Solid Foundation

Now, considering the descriptions in the chart above for both reputation and character, in your GIUY Success Journal, identify what people commonly say about you (your reputation) and then identify your principles/who you are at your core (your character). What are the consistencies or inconsistencies between the two?

_____

_____

_____

_____

SUMMARY OF THE WEEK

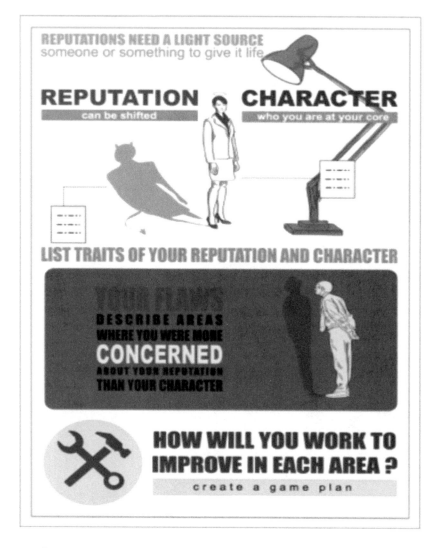

Order your copy of *Greatness Is Upon You* by the award-winning author of *The Secret to Success,* Eric Thomas, today! Visit www.etinspires.com/shop.

Welcome to
Breathe University™

A holistic approach to success, involving a series of
one on one intimate instructional sessions with
Inspirational Speaker and Life Strategist, Eric
Thomas, to help you transform your life in the areas
of: Finances, Relationships, Career Goals, Marriage
and more!

For more information contact:
info@BreatheUniversity.com or call 866-526-3978

SPIRIT REIGN PUBLISHING
A Division of Spirit Reign Communications